AMERICAN NAUTICAL
ART AND
ANTIQUES

Also by Jacqueline L. Kranz (with Frederick H. Kranz)

GARDENING INDOORS UNDER LIGHTS

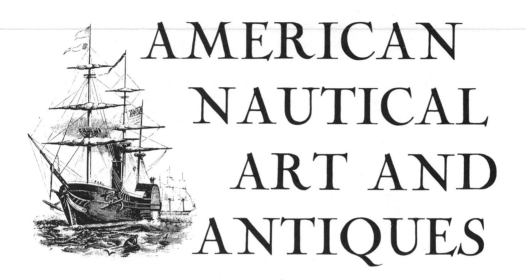

AMERICAN NAUTICAL ART AND ANTIQUES

BY JACQUELINE L. KRANZ

CROWN PUBLISHERS, INC.   NEW YORK

To Beth S. Fowler

who shared with me the fun of college,
the interest of working on the same newspaper,
the joy of our children and their development;
and especially the understanding that
is the elixir of life

Library of Congress Cataloging in Publication Data

Kranz, Jacqueline Longaker.
    American nautical art and antiques.

    Bibliography: p.
    Includes index.
    1. Naval art and science—Collectors and collecting.
I. Title.
    V745.K7   387.5'028   75-4559
    ISBN 0-517-51891-0

ACKNOWLEDGMENTS

My Deep Appreciation to
Mr. Michael Naab, Curator
Columbia River Maritime Museum
Astoria, Oregon

FOR HIS METICULOUS ATTENTION to detail in reading the manuscript for this book, for his unselfish service and long hours in correcting mistakes and misconceptions, for his many letters, and especially for his vast knowledge in the nautical field, which he used so unsparingly here so that others might profit by it.

My special thanks go to Rolf Klep, director of the Columbia River Maritime Museum, and to Revelle Carr, curator of the Mystic Seaport Museum, who were so generous with their time and knowledge. The personnel of all the museums I contacted during my research for this book—the Bath Marine Museum, The Mariners Museum in Newport News, the Philadelphia Maritime Museum, the San Francisco Maritime Museum, and the South Street Seaport Museum—cooperated fully, both in time and effort, to make this book both accurate and informative. I am also grateful to Elisabeth Helman and to the staff of the East Aurora Branch of the Buffalo and Erie County Public Library for the patient hunting up of materials; and to the New-York Historical Society for going out of their way to make their research materials available to me.

Arlene and Richard Orcutt deserve special thanks. Arlene, with her knowledge of prints and art, and Dick, who is a carver and has a vast amount of information about the sea and its life, have both been of immense help to me. Alongside the Orcutts, I have received outstanding support from the many dealers who have such a rich supply of nautical antiques. All have been helpful, from those who showed their wares in the prestigious antiques shows in New York City and the east, to the many others in small towns who unearthed their rare treasures. (The names and locations of all the museums and dealers to whom I am indebted are given in an appendix in the back of the book.)

My appreciative thanks go to my agent, Julie Fallowfield, and my editor, Kay Pinney, for their help and care in working with me. This book gained its present form through the efforts of *many* people: Neale Haley, my daughter, whose writing finesse and photographic skill have helped point the way; Beth S. Fowler, my lifelong friend, who can spell, edit, and encourage; Stewart K. Kranz, my son, whose sound knowledge of art and childhood absorption in making ship models awakened my interest in nautical treasures; Virginia Vidler, whose nose for news and photographic know-how unearthed many rare examples; Bonnie Drinkard and Gail B. Klépadlo, who provided their skillful typing; and Jacquetta M. Haley, who made those last-minute changes needed to give this book its final form.

CONTENTS

1

OUR PECULIAR HERITAGE

FOR CENTURIES, BEACHCOMBING HAS BEEN an exciting pastime. What has the sea left behind? Something of this same wonder is found in the collecting of nautical antiques. Who made this ditty box, so small, so artistically conceived, for the few personal possessions a sailor always takes on board? The anchor in the captain's garden—did it really save the ship, as they say it did? What a story! Can you feel the pride someone had in that silver cup? His cat-rig boat placed first in a race off Long Island in 1881—so it says, in cursive engraving.

Small wonder the collecting of nautical antiques has become so popular in the last few years. Collectors have discovered they are not gathering just beautifully made mementoes of an era that is past, but stories, too, stories of bravery, of courage, and of daring that are among the best of America's heritage. And it is not only individual collectors all over the United States—men, women, and children—who are seeking out these half-forgotten treasures that did not go down into the sea along with the ships, but governments and groups of citizens. They, too, have heard this call of the sea, and triumphantly they collect and preserve vessels that may have been sunk two hundred years ago, or are in such bad array that—were it not for a helping hand—they would go the way of the derelicts, as derelicts have gone from the time of the Phoenicians.

The establishment of maritime museums and the reconditioning of frigates, clippers, and schooners are a lively symbol of public interest in our seafaring heritage. Museums do preserve these ships, as well as the wheels that steered them, the nautical instruments that brought these wooden vessels through the storms; the bells, the lanterns, the handiwork that was a part of the long hours at sea. They are to be found on both the east and the west coasts, in the Great Lakes region, along the rivers that played their part in navigation, the Ohio and the Mississippi, the Columbia, and—of course—along that dangerous stretch of water between Montauk Point and Hell Gate, the inland sea that we call Long Island Sound.

One needs a guide because there are so many different facets to the collecting of nautical antiques: sheet music of a ballad written for a ship launching, with the ship engraved on the cover; paintings and prints, like the one in the Chicago Historical Society of Commodore Perry with his fully armed frigate, called *Carrying the Gospel to the Heathen*; medals; maps by which men sailed the treacherous passage around the Horn; half-models, the designs from which these gallant vessels were made.

To supply the need for such a guide, this book has been written. To the seasoned collector, it offers information he may not have seen, so vast and unexplored are the byways of the sea; to the novice, it points out the wealth of material that is his for the searching; to the general reader, it brings remembrance of a life that is half forgotten, of the romance of yesterday, gone and yet as ever present as the sea.

You do not need to be a seagoer to enjoy gifts from the deep. One of the most knowledgeable collectors of nautical antiques says, "I can't step on the deck of a sailboat, if there's the slightest roll, without getting seasick—yet even the smallest piece of scrimshaw speaks to me of the loneliness, the monotony, and the grandeur of those who sailed the seas, as strongly as the finely carved eagle that once graced the pilothouse of a steamship. There are no trifles in nautical antiques."

Looking for nautical antiques on land is a surer way of keeping them than bringing them up from the sea, where the greatest abundance lies. But both methods are being tried. Few of us are adept at deep-sea diving, or charting and claiming wrecks of the past, but many are learning the needed skills. Moreover, there are laws that certain of the seas' treasures belong to the government, to be displayed for the good of the people.

1. A bone model flanked by plates that came to this country from across the sea. *Frank F. Sylvia Antiques*

2. Square-riggers and clippers in the China trade started our nation on a million-dollar wave of prosperity. They not only stopped in ports like this, but brought back pictures and prints to show what the mysterious East was really like. *Hilbert Brothers Collection*

3. Trifles? Not at all. Historic documents of days that are past: visitor tags from the launching celebrations for submarines, and the manual charting the difficulties of sailing the Great Lakes, which, doughty sea captains claim, were far more difficult than the sea. *Virginia Vidler*

When the winds roar, and your own small craft—be it yacht, canoe, or dory—is snugly in dock for the winter, it is pleasant to fondle an old divider and to chart a course to your particular fancy—and, as you pause, to look with appreciation at the fine old print of a square-rigger hanging on your wall. Deep in your heart, like many of us, you may cherish a love of the sea and marvel at the romance and tragedy that ride its waves. Small wonder, then, that you seek reminders of these adventures for your own private delight. The love of things nautical can be a rewarding hobby.

4. Nautical treasures become the focal point in the offices and homes of collectors. Among the nautical antiques on this hobby wall are a half-model of a three-masted schooner, a pilothouse eagle, and a lacquered board for the carved ivory chess set that was brought to this country on a clipper ship.

5. A starboard sidelight from an old sailing ship, an octant of yesteryear, and a duck decoy (which attracts decorators as well as sportsmen) are the kinds of things that surface in the search for nautical antiques. *Orcutt Collection*

Sometimes this nautical field may lead to glory and unusual achievements, as it did with the young girl who grew up loving her grandfather's sextant and sea barometer. She loved them so much that she learned to navigate. While still in her twenties, she sailed alone in a secondhand boat with only three hundred feet of sail from Maine to an island in the West Indies. Her accomplishment made the headlines and gained for her the respect of all sea lovers.

This book will not make you a navigator at sea, but with it as a guide you can sail confidently into one of the newest and most fascinating of collecting hobbies, and discover the joy of the sea more surely than you did as a child when you put a conch shell to your ear.

WHERE DO YOU FIND NAUTICAL TREASURES?

"Where do you find these nautical relics?" is the question most often asked by beginning collectors. Then they are likely to add: "I've never seen one anywhere."

This may be a favorable omen for the bargain-hunting nautical collector. It follows that, having come upon an unappreciated treasure, you are likely to have something of monetary value. While we were looking over an auction catalog of nautical antiques, a museum curator said: "I did not go. I knew that the prices would be beyond our reach."

And yet, a short time later, I found a whaling scroll for $7.50 in a Greenwich, Connecticut, shop. The cloth was handwoven. On it an excellent artist had portrayed scenes from Yankee whaling days, including the kind of home where wives waited and watched for their returning mariners—sometimes through years of patient pacing around the white-fenced widow's walk atop the house, whence they could see far out to sea.

To get an overall view of the variety and scope of articles that may be classed as "nautical antiques" or—as Curator Michael Naab of the Columbia River Maritime Museum points out—the also interesting "nautical objects" of later vintage, you should visit some of the fascinating marine museums around the country. Founded for the most part in the 1960s, they have played an important part in awakening interest in nautical antiques, as well as finding, identifying, preserving, and displaying the vanishing heritage of our seafaring past.

These museums have been in a favored position, Director Rolf Klep of the Columbia River Maritime Museum pointed out. "A museum is the first place people think of when pondering what to do with a family keepsake. They like the idea of a secure harbor for these things."

The individual collector of nautical antiques would not have this particular advantage, but it does give him a clue about where to look first. That is at home, in the attic and storage bins, at the prints on the wall, in the old family photograph albums, and perhaps in the sewing basket, where my own grand-

WAVES IN SILENCE REST

6. Waves rest in silence over the deeps that secrete the skeletons of the thousands of vessels lost since the days when man first ventured on a bounding deck to challenge the unknown. This statue at Hampton Beach, New Hampshire, is dedicated to men who went down at sea. With them lies the greatest of all stores of nautical antiques. *Photograph by Edward W. Vidler*

mother's darning egg, viewed with a knowledgeable eye, turned out to be a piece of scrimshaw.

Mr. Klep mentioned other sources that are as open to private collectors as they are to museum directors: antiques shops, auctions, flea markets, the currently popular garage sales. And not the least important—the beaches.

"Our eagle figurehead was found on the Oregon coast in two parts," Mr. Klep said. The eagle, sanded down to a soft, pale golden shade, is neatly joined in two lengthwise parts like the halves of an orange or a walnut meat. The beachcomber who found this prize picked up half one day, and, to his delight, found the other half buried in the sand a few days later. You need not have a professional title to follow the example of these dedicated men in charge of maritime museums.

And then there is the sea itself. Scuba diving is now taught as a part of physical education in many high schools and colleges. Youthful seekers are div-

7. "I would like to find a good wheel," one museum curator said to me. His wish is shared by many a man. Sometimes you do find one at an antiques show or shop. *Nina Hellman Antiques*

8. The sea itself sometimes washes treasures onto the beach, as it did this eagle, found in two pieces on two different days. The construction usually used in figureheads secured the two pieces: an extension on one (the tenon) and a socket on the other (the mortise). A wooden peg through both parts adds to the strength of the joint. *Columbia River Maritime Museum*

ing to see what they can find. Off the shores of Texas, they discovered such rich treasure in a sunken Spanish galleon that the state legislature appropriated funds to have the vessel raised and restored.

A group of scuba divers brought out of the depths of Lake Erie, very near the site of the fort that gave the village its name—Fort Erie, in Canada—parts of an old vessel: long spikes, hardware (see Ill. 9), traces of wood that had been buried in the sand, and, quite dramatically, a cannonball. Was this the remnant of a ship sunk in the War of 1812? It could well have been. The shards of pottery resembled late-eighteenth-century crocks.

Another group of helmet divers, those wearing the heavy older type of gear divers use for walking on the bottom, brought out of Lake Ontario guns that

9. Today a new era conquers the deep as divers plunge to the ocean floor to pick at wrecks. Here are the finds of a single diver, William De Fries, from a single vessel in Lake Erie. A shard of pottery dates the wreck to 1812. He brought up spikes, a cheek block, and even a horseshoe. *Photographed by William De Fries, De Fries Collection*

dated back to the French and Indian Wars. This valuable booty went to a museum.

As Bill De Fries once said to me, "You just never know. Four of us found an iron chain, hand-forged and old. It must have been seventy-five feet or more in length. It was hard to get it up to our boat, and when we did, we had to let it go—it was so heavy that just a small portion of it made the boat begin to sink. Possibly, sometime—with a bigger boat . . ."

Another new subject taught in some universities is ocean engineering; it brings to light startling facts about old ships and battles. For example, the University of Rhode Island's Department of Ocean Engineering has discovered a British fleet that scuttled itself in Narragansett Bay during the Revolutionary War. In dives off Aquidneck Island the frigates *Cerberus, Lark,* and *Orpheus* have been discovered, and some of the larger artifacts brought to the surface.

A

10 A & B. Sometimes you find nautical treasures at antiques shows amid Tiffany lamps. This picture by Bailey (*A*) was displayed in the booth of Eleanor Mulligan. Others are found at rummage sales, auctions, or, like the *Elsie* (*B*) shown here, at a commission mart. (*B*), *Cornelia Black, Westchester Commission Mart Antiques*

B

11. You may even find a nautical antique on the top shelf of the kitchen cupboard. That's where this tobacco jar crowned with a French sailor and decorated with square-riggers was found. Owned for two hundred years by the Warren Long family, it is now in the author's collection.

12. Marine museums often have shops where unusual items appear. Who would expect to find a half-horse, half-dragon figurehead for sale? Yet here one is in the city of New York at the South Street Seaport Museum shop.

The work on the sunken ships is already being described as the most significant archeological project ever undertaken in North America.

Early ships known to have been sunk off Florida, Texas, and Virginia have aroused so much interest among nautical antiques enthusiasts that great efforts are being made to locate them and bring up the long-hidden booty: old gold coins, nautical instruments, pewterware, cooking utensils—all mementoes of days long past.

But those who frequent neither flea markets nor underwater coves can find treasures in the more normal avenues of trade. Antiques dealers in big shops and little are awakening to this nautical interest that is sweeping the country. In a small antiques shop in Dunkirk, New York, on Lake Erie, I saw —priced at twenty-eight dollars—a banjo-type barometer in a well-carved case that could have been used on an old vessel. In a prestigious antiques show in New York's Coliseum I counted in the many booths more than 150 nautical antiques for sale. Many were extremely rare, of the highest museum quality. Others were so reasonably priced that two or three of them changed hands several times before the show opened. There were both variety and richness among the nautical antiques displayed. They indicated what an open field this still is for those who want just a single piece or hope to start a collection.

Well-authenticated pieces are naturally expensive, but they are never a poor investment. The source is limited, and interest in them is rising—and rising. Look hard, like the scuba divers; you never know what you may turn up.

WHAT DO YOU CALL THEM?

One of the by-products of collecting nautical antiques is learning the vernacular of the sea. Looking at a harbor picture, you will come to say: "What tremendous *vessels*"—not, "Have you ever seen such *boats*?" Listen to the matter-of-fact comments of the museum directors. They always say *vessels*. It is the landlubbers—most of us—who slip into the familiar usage, "boats."

Vessel is the correct term for all types of watercraft. It covers everything from oceangoing liners to small dories. *Boat* is used only for small craft—yachts, dories, canoes, and the like; *ship* is applied to larger vessels. It may seem a small distinction, but it is important for the nautical collector to know the vocabulary.

Nevertheless, *boat* has been the favorite in the nation's vocabulary for a long time. In the colonies, it was often used to apply to vessels in general, even though the distinction was well known at the time. In an advertisement in the *Constitutional Gazette*, October 7, 1775, we find one Peter Arell in some terminological conflict as he defends his honor in the matter of the destruction of a certain "boat"—or "barge" or "ship."

> Boat Builders—City of New York. Peter Arell of said city Boat Builder, being duly sworn upon the Holy Evangelists of Almighty God, deposeth and said, that the boat or barge which Mr. Henry Sheaf was lately building for his Majesty's ship *Asia* and destroyed by some person or persons unknown to this deponent and that he neither advised, aided, or abetted in destroying said boat, and this department further saith that he hath not been in Henry Sheaf's workshop for four years last past and further saith not.

As a collector of nautical antiques (especially one who likes ship models—

American Clipper Ship - 1850   *Norm Maffei*

13. Is it a ship or a boat? The distinctions are definite among seamen. Whenever you are uncertain, use the word "vessel"—it covers everything that floats. The term "boat" does not apply to large vessels, although landlubbers use it freely. This clipper is a ship, not a boat. *Gibson's Antiques*

Fig. 1. Three-masted schooner. *Drawing by Louisette Barrett*

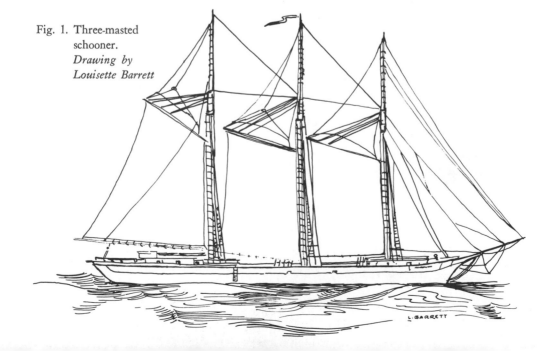

14. Ships were usually square-rigged. There are generally many small squarish sails on each mast. The sails appear to reach across the vessel from side to side. In this painting by Oswald Brett of the *Wavertree* fighting heavy seas, only a few sails are set, but you can see the narrow yards to which the sailors clung when setting sails. *South Street Seaport Museum*

and where is the collector who doesn't?), you will become even more knowledgeable about *rigs*. There are many variations in rigs, as H. I. Chappelle, the great authority on sailing ships, points out. Nine are considered basic. An excellent pamphlet prepared by the Peabody Museum of Salem on these nine types, with illustrations in silhouette by Charles G. Davis, is worth having in hand. You can recognize the sloop, with its one mast, with fore-and-aft rig. The same

15. This five-masted schooner, the *Jennie Flood Kreuger,* shows the rhythmic simplicity of the schooner rig. The lower sail on each mast is large and appears to reach toward both bow and stern, which earns it the name fore-and-aft rig. *Courtesy of The Mariners Museum, Newport News, Virginia*

rig also made the schooner successful. Few men are needed to operate it. Square-rigged vessels take more men.

The bark combines both rigs. It is a three-masted vessel, with foremast (the first one) and mainmast (the second one) both square-rigged with yards. The mizzenmast (the third one, closest to the stern) is fore-and-aft-rigged, with a gaff-topsail.

The barkentine was a vessel with more of the schooner's fore-and-aft rigging and less of the square-rigger's. Only the foremast was square-rigged. This was made in three spars, but all the other masts were of the schooner type. One or two schooner-rigged masts could be added, making a four- or five-masted vessel. It was popular for its ability to make speed and its easy handling with fewer men.

At first, the many new terms may sound difficult, but wait until you come upon a schooner model—the words will glow. You will know the names of the three masts and what a fore-and-aft rig is, and even a gaff. You will also learn to speak offhandedly about "port" and "starboard" sides of the vessel: "port" on the left as you face the bow, opposed to the right or "starboard" side. My young son used to explain it this way: "You come into port, and that's the port side. The other side looks out on the stars. That's starboard."

Happy landings! Learning a new tongue can prove delightful.

16. Inland, a steamer is a steamboat, but on the open seas it is a steamship. This side-wheeler is the *J. Putnam Bradley. Kenneth E. Snow Antiques*

The Raft.

17. This raft is a vessel, and it has all the comforts of a home. In fact, it is almost a houseboat. It sailed the Mississippi with passengers and freight before the days of the steamboat. The smaller vessels tend to be called boats. You say tugboat, ferryboat, and lifeboat naturally, and are correct. A dory, a canoe, and a yacht are also boats. A submarine? It is a boat too. *America Illustrated*

18. Canoes are the original boats of America. Whether hewn from logs, like this 1820 example from the Northwest, or carefully made of birch bark; whether from the Chesapeake Bay area or the Great Lakes, all are collectors' items. Their form has persisted, but the skill that went into their making has almost vanished. *Columbia River Maritime Museum*

2

SHIPS WORTH REMEMBERING

THANKS TO THE MARINE MUSEUMS and the United States government, the neophyte collector and the experienced one as well have the opportunity close at hand to discover for themselves the genuine nature of nautical antiques. And all of us can become volunteers and participate in the very process of restoration.

Today, you can walk the decks of the frigate *Constitution,* which fought the Barbary pirates in the War of 1812; you can board the only surviving whaler, the *Charles W. Morgan* (see Ill. 19), which for eighty years was one of the most successful of ships in "being where the whales were"; you can go aboard the *Sherman Zwicker,* a typical Grand Banks fishing schooner, and see for yourself why schooners played such an important part in building America. What a cargo they could carry with only an eight-man crew!

Walking the decks of these old ships is exciting—a pleasure that many millions of Americans enjoy each year. In the last decade or two, marine museums and national, state, and local governments have turned with vigor to our seafaring, riverboat past. Out of the sea, the lakes, and riverbeds they have rescued half-forgotten vessels and restored them for us to study and enjoy. Maritime museums have been opened in old coastal shipbuilding towns, not only on the east and west coasts, but in the interior of the country, on the Great Lakes, and by many of our mighty rivers, such as the Mississippi and the Columbia.

19. Model of the *Charles W. Morgan,* the only surviving whaler. Ship models rank high as collectible nautical antiques. Their value lies in how accurately each one is made to scale, how well it is rigged. *Photograph by Bern C. Ritchie & Co.*

It is hard to realize what these old vessels meant to our country until you board one of them. You step back into a time when ships, not motor cars, were the sinews of our national life, and by some strange osmosis you put down roots into our nation's past. It is all to the good that governments and museums and enlightened citizens have joined in seeking out these vessels that were not lost in the sea.

Few of us, however, stop to think how expensive it is to keep these old vessels in the water. It helps if you happen to know someone who has a small boat or yacht. A friend of mine who loves to sail with her husband sighs deeply each spring as they make plans to take the small sailboat out of storage for the summer's fun.

"You can't imagine how much time you have to spend just maintaining it," she says. "There's always something more that needs to be done."

When I mention the fleets that so many of the marine museums proudly dock near their buildings, she just shakes her head. "I wonder how they manage," she says.

The next time you board one of these restored ships, stop for a moment to think what it costs to maintain the vessel. You'll feel indebted to the museum, possibly enough to join. Whether the restoration is an old ferry or a veteran

20. Standing beneath the bow of
    a mighty sailing vessel at
    South Street Seaport, you
    sense the dedication of the
    New Yorkers who are strug-
    gling to create a panorama of
    the past in a fleet of vessels
    that actually put to sea. Here
    the bow of the tiny *Pioneer*
    hardly obscures the *Ambrose*
    lightship at all.

21. It has been nearly a century
    since San Franciscans could
    look up at the sky and see
    silhouetted against it the
    beauty of tall slender masts
    the way they appear today at
    the San Francisco Maritime
    State Historic Park. Here at
    anchor is the *C. A. Thayer.*

22. For a moment, standing there on the pier at South Street Seaport, you can feel as a seaman did a century ago when he viewed the vessel that shortly would put to sea with him on board—to be gone for months or years. What excitement raced through him as he paused for a moment to look up at the bowsprit of *his* ship!

23. Nor are steamboats forgotten at nautical museums. Here, the *Alexander Hamilton* visits South Street Seaport, berthed beside the square-rigged and gaff-rigged sailing vessels. The *Alexander Hamilton* is owned by the Railroad Pier Company of Atlantic Highlands, New Jersey.

24. When South Street Seaport is restored in all its authenticity, there will be nautical antiques from every type of vessel important in America's past. Tourists and lovers of the sea, antiquers and historians, will be able not only to climb aboard the old vessels but to examine fascinating displays. This diorama shows what the completed project at South Street will look like.

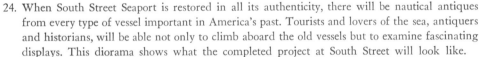

25. The tug *Sadie Ross,* one of the last of the coal-burners, is anchored at Newburyport, Massachusetts. Here she rides, in all her "splendor," beneath a vessel built to resemble the *Flying Cloud* (though not to scale). *Photograph by Edward W. Vidler*

whaler, it is an important means of telling thousands something of our past.

Of all the ships afloat the most distinguished is the *Constitution*, maintained by the United States government in the Boston Navy Yard. She was one of the ships that the Congress ordered built when the United States first became a nation.

Drums rolled and patriots cheered when the five frigates authorized by the Congress in 1777 went down the ways. It would have been impossible for those early citizens to realize that one of those five, the U.S.S. *Constitution*, would survive the years to become the oldest warship afloat. Her career was a series of daring feats, climaxed in 1812 by her encounter with the British ship of the line, the *Guerrière*, six hundred miles east of Boston. Captain Isaac Hull was in command at that famous victory. Though only the crews saw the battle, it became the most widely portrayed event of our early history. The collector will find it not only in paintings and in prints but also in scrimshaw and embroidery.

About to be dismantled, the *Constitution* might not have survived to inspire such long-lasting veneration if Oliver Wendell Holmes had not rallied the nation to her support with his poem "Old Ironsides." Funds poured in, and she began her second career as the most popular naval attraction in the country. To her public she is more often *Old Ironsides* than the *Constitution*.

Because there are so few old sailing vessels left, many carefully constructed replicas have been made. For example, in St. Petersburg, Florida, there's the replica of the *Bounty*. Moored at the municipal pier, it is popular with tourists. In 1960, Metro-Goldwyn-Mayer used the ship in *Mutiny on the Bounty*, and after the filming turned it over to be enjoyed by the people.

Some of the old ships in museums were literally brought up from the sea or a lake or river, just as the many restored ships abroad have been. Possibly the most famous is the *Philadelphia*, a continental gondola built in 1777, which sank that same year in Lake Champlain. Raised and restored, she is now in the Smithsonian Institution in Washington, D.C.

Lovers of steamboats can also find restorations. There is the *W. P. Snyder*,

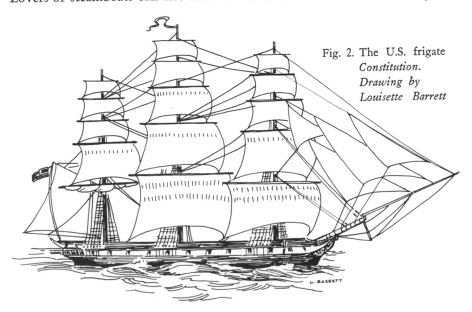

Fig. 2. The U.S. frigate *Constitution*. *Drawing by Louisette Barrett*

L. BARRETT

26. The *Constitution* was a heroine of the War of 1812. She became the most painted frigate of the American navy. Any rendering of her—on board, canvas, paper, bone, or pottery—is in demand. The original watercolor is in the United States Naval Museum.

27. You can collect the life-sized vessels of an age that is gone—not in your backyard, but in your memory or with your camera. The quest can take you all over the nation, but begin at home, for a long-forgotten vessel may lie in a river nearby. At Wiscasset, Maine, the hull of an abandoned schooner, the *Hasper*, lies waiting. Will it continue to rot, or be saved?

in Marietta, Ohio, anchored in the river. It is advertised as one of the last of the Mark Twain side-wheelers. And at Shelburne, Vermont, there is the *Ticonderoga*, the last of the Lake Champlain steamships. There just wouldn't be any "lasts" if it were not for historically minded people who do their best to preserve them.

The *Balclutha,* now moored in the San Francisco Maritime State Historic Park* in the Fisherman's Wharf area, was saved from destruction by the efforts of the museum and the citizenry in 1954, and restored to her original state as a Cape Horn square-rigger. The government moved in to help; money allotted to parks was applied to transforming Fisherman's Wharf from a rundown street to a parklike area, the delight and wonder of tourists and townsfolk alike. Combined government and museum efforts have brought more ships, and the skyline today—with its silhouette of masts—speaks nostalgically of the 1850s, when San Francisco was one of the most popular ports of the world.

If you are a camera enthusiast, old ships offer ways of learning more about nautical antiques. Pay attention to detail as you frame the photographic shots, noting fittings, masts, rigging. You will find the process a valuable help in collecting nautical antiques.

"THE FASTEST WAY TO GET TO NEW YORK." These words were once emblazoned on a poster on the rear end of a New York, New Haven, and Hartford commuter train. The means of achieving this marvel of transportation was unclear. Certainly not by rail. But the words—there was as much magic in them as in the early 1800s, when Robert Fulton's discovery brought about a commercially successful steamboat. To think of a boat so unbelievably fast! The number of passengers carried paled in significance beside the length of the time it took to make the trip. Record passages made headlines. America had entered on the age of speed and, then as now, speed was her goddess.

Those who could not gather on the banks of the Hudson or at the boarding dock at the foot of Cortland Street where the *Clermont* left on Friday at nine in the morning—to arrive in Albany Saturday at nine "in the afternoon"—had to content themselves with pictured departures, sailings, and arrivals. It was not long before artists and printmakers rose to the occasion. Turning out paintings and engravings to meet the demand, all unwittingly they were also producing collectors' items.

Robert Fulton was, in many ways, the man of the hour. Others had sought to propel a boat by steam, but they had not been able to make it commercially feasible. Fulton added—to the qualities of inventor—business acumen and the right associate, Chancellor Livingston, to make his steamboat, the *Clermont,* a success. Coming as it did just as the United States was turning toward the unsettled and unclaimed West, his contribution met a very real need.

From the very start of steam navigation, the Hudson River was a racetrack. Newspapers recorded the exceptional times the steamboats made in the run from New York to Albany. Skilled river captains basked in having made a record time in the vessels they commanded. Races were a part of river life

---

* The more popular term "Fisherman's Wharf" will generally be used hereafter in this book, but it should be remembered that the restorations are actually in the state park.

28. At San Francisco Maritime State Historic Park near Fisherman's Wharf, one of the world's great restorations, the steam schooner *Wapama* (left) awaits the tramp of modern feet as it once did those of seamen. There too is the *C. A. Thayer* (below), the three-masted schooner that once sailed the rugged West Coast to carry lumber for a score of uses to a score of ports. *San Francisco Maritime Museum*

29. Robert Fulton, whose steamship *Clermont* sails in the memory of every man, whether he is a sailor or not. *Good and Hutchinson, Inc.*

30. Model of a steam engine of the type used on the *Mary Powell*, beloved craft on the Hudson River for fifty years. *Mystic Seaport photograph, Mystic, Connecticut*

whenever one steamboat came up with another—in fair weather, of course, but also in storm and flood tide, in darkness and wintry blast.

Years later, the *Mary Powell* became the sweetheart of the Hudson River Day Line. She plied the river for sixty years. When she was sold for scrap, financiers vied for parts of her. Henry Ford bought her remarkable engine (see Ill. 30) for his Dearborn Museum, but a replica of it is on display in the museum at Mystic Seaport, Connecticut. J. P. Morgan bought the two gilt bells from her mast to grace the gateposts of his Highland Falls estate. Lesser known collectors paid high prices for other parts. Even the wood from her hull was preserved, built into the Mary Powell Cottage, near Kingston, New York, her last port, where the museum houses her steering wheel. The nameboard, *Mary Powell*, is installed in the cottage.

For a time, only her two tall smokestacks remained near the remnants of the hull—an irony, in that these were her claims to fame in her heyday: not one, but two smokestacks—stately and high—the most popular feature of one of the marvels of the nineteenth century, the steamship. Finally, in 1938, a collector rescued them and carried them away as his memento of a glorious era.

Another marvel of the times, the photograph, added prestige to the claims

of the *Mary Powell*. In her original salon hung photographs made by Mathew Brady of such eminent men as John James Audubon, James Gordon Bennett, and Washington Irving.

In addition to the Day Line, the Hudson River Night Line made scheduled trips to Albany. The glamour of these ships is conveyed in a description by a visitor from South America, one Domingo Sarmiento:

> They are floating palaces, three stories in height with galleries and roofs for promenading. Gold shines in the capitals and architecture of the thousand columns which, as in the *Isaac Newton*, flank monstrous halls, capable of containing the Senate and the House of Representatives. Artistically draped hangings of damask hide staterooms for five hundred passengers, and there is a colossal dining room with an endless table of polished mahogany and service porcelain and plate for a thousand guests.

Robert Fulton and Chancellor Livingston had marked the Mississippi as *the* steamboat river of the country. However, even they did not foresee the time in the 1850s when two thousand steamers and more would speed from Saint Paul to the delta in New Orleans, more interested in getting there fast than in taking care of passengers and freight.

Two years after they had launched their *Clermont* on the Hudson, Livingston and Fulton sent one of their capable young engineers to plan and supervise the building of a steamboat in Pittsburgh, then the gateway to the West. On that planning trip, Nicholas Roosevelt envisioned the completed project as a pioneer event that would also provide a very fine honeymoon trip for himself and his bride. But by the time the *New Orleans* was ready to be launched two years later—even then, because of flood conditions, before she was quite finished—Mrs. Roosevelt was about to become a mother. As dedicated to faith in the new steam-powered river traffic as her husband, she was determined to go along on the initial voyage to New Orleans.

Problems developed the moment the craft anchored at Louisville. Threatening Indians were frightened away only by the mysterious fire and smoke that came out of the stack, but they were not alone in their fright. As the ship lay at anchor, steam escaping from the engine terrified the local inhabitants into near panic—they were afraid it was the end of the world. But the real "event" was the birth of the Roosevelt baby, after which they decided to stay tied up for a while before continuing the trip down the river.

When steam was got up to set forth again, the first hurdle was the Ohio rapids just below Louisville. The river was still at flood stage, but a skilled pilot was at the wheel. To the utter astonishment of the crowds that lined the banks expecting the worst, the little boat headed straight into the rapids at full speed—and came through unscathed. That single accomplishment may be said to have brought steam to the Ohio River.

The Roosevelts did not have long to glow in the achievement. They were

31. Both the grandeur and the practicality of the steamboat were realized on the Mississippi. Forgotten was the time when it took 150 days to pole a flatboat from New Orleans to Saint Louis. This picture (called "Wooding Up") emphasizes the vast amounts of wood needed for firing the boilers. *America Illustrated*

not much farther down the river when the whole boat began to tremble and shake. Spurts of water rose high. Trees toppled. The superstitious felt sure the river gods were taking their revenge on this strange chugging boat invading their waters. Nor did the commotion soon let up. (Later, they discovered they had experienced the tremors from the New Madrid earthquake that shook the entire Mississippi Valley.) Landmarks and the channel disappeared, making all Roosevelt's carefully prepared charts of no value. Fire broke out in the ship's galley because the cook had put the freshly chopped kindling too close to the stove, but the crew managed to put it out. From that time on, they had to chop fuel for the boilers from the forests on the riverbanks.

One night the steamboat was moored by securely fastening a rope to a tree on an island in the river. The next morning the rope was still taut, stretching down into the water, but the island had disappeared. It was scarcely the type of journey that a doting father would have chosen for his firstborn.

The tremors, the geysers, the baths of muddy water from sudden eddies and spray, gradually slackened, and by the time the *New Orleans* reached Natchez, the tremors finally disappeared completely. All that lay ahead were muddy water and a flooding river. The captain of the *New Orleans* was undaunted. She was bound for New Orleans, and she would go to New Orleans. They did stop at Natchez, however, to take stock, to make plans, and best of all to pick up a cargo of cotton. A trusting plantation owner, in spite of warnings from his friends, decided to send it to New Orleans in this new boat.

With a paying load in the hold, the *New Orleans* steamed on. She arrived

32. A fine model of a flat-bottom Mississippi riverboat. Its promenade decks were the height of dazzling popularity in the 1850s. *Photograph by Bern C. Ritchie & Co.*

in the Gulf city on January 12, 1812. With flood, fire, earthquake, stamina, and courage, proof of the power of steam had been brought to the Mississippi.

And the *New Orleans?* She quickly went into passenger and freight service between Natchez and New Orleans.

Should you find an engraving or a painting of the *Savannah,* made at the time of her historic journey across the Atlantic in 1819, you will be the only person known to own such a prize. There *must* be some contemporary representations extant! Many, of course, have been made since.

The *Savannah* was the first vessel to use steam in crossing the Atlantic. Not throughout the entire crossing, it is true. There were wide expanses of the ocean where the winds were right and she could sail along as all others had sailed since the earliest crossings. For fuel she had seventy-five tons of coal and twenty-five cords of wood, which permitted between eighty and ninety hours of steaming time on the whole voyage. As it turned out, eighteen hours was the ship's longest period under steam during the trip.

As the *Savannah* neared the coast of England, smoke belching, she was chased by a British revenue cutter whose master thought she was on fire. The *Savannah* confidently pursued her way. She did not stop until her would-be rescuers sent a shot across her bow.

Thousands watched her as she steamed up the Mersey in England. Newspapers pondered that "this steam operation may, in some manner, be connected with the ambitious views of the United States." The *Times* of London reported, "The *Savannah,* a steam vessel, recently arrived at Liverpool from America, the first vessel of that kind which ever crossed the Atlantic."

Any portrayal of the *Savannah* (see Fig. 3) can be positively identified by the innovations that brought her the honor. Marestier, describing her, said she had the appearance of an ordinary sailing ship with three masts, about three hundred tons.

The rigging does not differ materially. The spanker and lower staysails are held by gaffs and spars like trisails. The forward stay of the main mast is divided; the two parts are led to the bulwarks foreward of the foremast stays. This is intended to prevent the rigging from catching fire.

Between the foremast and the mainmast were the steamship innovations said to have been designed by Captain Moses Rogers: the collapsible paddle wheel and the swivel smokestack. These can be clearly seen in Marestier's drawing. (The iron frame with a canvas cover that was designed to protect the paddle wheel is not shown in the drawing.) The smokestack was fitted with an elbow at the top so that, as the smoke and sparks came out, they could be turned away from the sails. This was a unique feature. So were the collapsible paddle wheels. Marestier described them this way:

> They are 16 feet in diameter. There are two on each side of the boat. They can be dismantled in 15 or 20 minutes. The spokes fit into one another, which greatly reduces the bulk of the wheels. The buckets are 4.65 feet long, 2.72 feet high. They are not rectangular like the buckets of a steamboat, because their outside corners have been cut off.

When the *Savannah* was built, no one, not even the ship's owner, Colonel Stevens of New York, had too much faith in a steam engine to propel a ship. By designing her so the paddle wheels could be quickly dismantled, the theory was that the captain could quickly turn to the safe and proven power of sail. In fact, not long after her epic journey across the Atlantic by steam, the *Savannah* was reconverted into a sailing ship.

Another reason that there might well be hidden portraits of the *Savannah* around somewhere was Captain Rogers's well-developed sense of publicity. He sounds more like a skilled presidential adviser than the great skipper he proved to be in the early 1800s. He used every channel to promote his ship. None was more ingenious than the excursion trip he arranged to take the President of the

Fig. 3. The only contemporary picture of the *Savannah* known to us today is a drawing made by a Frenchman, Marestier, who was sent to America to study the new steamboats. This illustration, made by Louisette Barrett, is based on the Marestier picture and shows the unique removable right-angled smokestack designed to direct sparks away from the sails.

33. A steamship in Portland, Maine, harbor in the days when sailing craft abounded. *Gleason's Pictorial Drawing-Room Companion*

United States on the ship's maiden voyage to Tybee Light (off Savannah) and return.

Captain Rogers knew that President James Monroe was making a goodwill tour of the South. The President was in Charleston, South Carolina. Rogers's ship was anchored in its home port—Savannah, Georgia. What better publicity than to have the President take a trip on the famous ship before she started across the Atlantic? Rogers set out for Charleston to invite the President and his entourage for a short run down the coast to Georgia on board the *Savannah*.

But the President dared not accept. He knew the fervor with which each southern state defended its honor. South Carolinians would possibly be offended, and his political chances damaged, should he thus leave their state. So he declined. It was a quite different matter to accept such an invitation in Georgia, so President Monroe and his party boarded this strange new vessel there, and under Captain Rogers's direction greatly enjoyed the all-day excursion to Tybee Light and back. Would a man so conscious as was Captain Rogers of the value of putting his ship before the public have ignored the more common vehicles of publicity: the commemorative dishes, the delicately shaded aquatint, a painting or two by one of the well-known marine artists? It doesn't seem that he would. Yet today these are but antiques of the imagination, waiting to be found.

Actually, two ships from England, *Syrus* and *Great Eastern* (see Ills. 34 and 35) were the first to cross the Atlantic wholly on steam, from Liverpool to New York. Though the *Syrus* ran out of coal and had to burn woodwork and spars to maintain steam pressure, she made it in eighteen days and ten hours.

The *New York Herald* pointed out, "This epic day opens quite a new era in the whole philosophy of Commerce, the arts and social life."

As steamships developed and became commonplace, they added an element of excitement and chance to the lives of many people. Ships of the Cunard Line often did better than their American competitors in crossing time. Large sums of money were bet on the outcomes of various crossings; and, as one writer put it: ". . . the race for speed and ocean supremacy from 1840 to 1892 began to leave behind trails of tragedy afloat, and ruin ashore."

Creating as much excitement as other waterways, if not more, was the man-made Erie Canal, "hand-built" a century and a half ago. For almost a hundred years, from 1825 to 1919, the canal was *the* throughway from New York to the Great Lakes and beyond. In 1859, some nineteen thousand boats passed through the locks at Lockport (see Ill. 40). For many travelers these locks were a wonder almost equal to Niagara Falls. For the boats and crews, they were a challenge to pride. So frequent were fistfights between captains of rafts and barges to settle the question of who should go through first that newspapers issued warnings to passengers. Cautioned the *Niagara Courier:*

> We feel it is our duty as publishing journalists, however unpleasant it may be, to put the travelling community on their guard to avoid taking passage in either of the lines of packet boats plying between the cities of Buffalo and Rochester. The belligerent attitude these boats have towards each other in attacking the respective crews with bludgeons and missiles renders it totally unsafe for passengers to travel in them.

Preferring novelty, excitement, and speed to safety, passengers continued to travel the canal route. Luxuriously equipped packet boats, often named for famous clippers, made the trip from New York to Buffalo in the "incredibly

34. *The Great Eastern* had an iron hull, miracle in the days of wooden ships. This original picture, put out by the owners, illustrates the glamour of early steamships. *Hilbert Brothers Collection*

PICTORIAL HISTORY

OF

THE GREAT EASTERN

STEAM-SHIP.

London:
PUBLISHED BY W. H. SMITH AND SON, 186 STRAND, LONDON.

FROM THE GREAT EASTERN.

35. Ship advertisements sometimes contain unusual prints of ships. Shown here is the cover of a pictorial booklet on *The Great Eastern*. Illustrated pamphlets on ships are almost museum pieces. *Hilbert Brothers Collection*

36. Tall stacks were built before the era of forced drafts—sometimes not only to draw off smoke from the fireboxes but to serve as dramatic decoration. This engraving depicts a scene at Fort Brown, Texas. *Harper's Weekly, 1861*

37. The Erie Canal was a great tourist attraction, second only to Niagara Falls. Early prints and paintings of what has been called New York State's first throughway are not common, and are in great demand. This ink sketch pictures an 1825 canalboat with passengers on the cabin roof. The steersman used a horn to signal an approaching town. *Efner Collection, City Historian's Office, Schenectady, New York*

38. Grain boats on the Erie Canal. *American Illustrated*

39. Little two-masted schooners resembling this model were a common sight on the Erie Canal as they carried cargo to other vessels. *Orcutt Collection*

40. Prints of the locks of the Erie Canal at Lockport, New York, come in at least two versions. One, dated 1825, illustrated here, has ordinary buildings along the sides. Another type—you might find examples—was made in Germany and showed the buildings as romantic castles. *Bartlett's American Scenery at The Canal Museum, Syracuse, New York*

short" time of six or seven days. Whiskey was almost as cheap on the canal as water. During the time the canal was being constructed, contractors would buy it for $4.50 a barrel to distribute to the men as a work incentive.

As far as is known, not even a replica remains of one of the old grain boats or packets that plied the canal. But collectors find many other artifacts to remind them of New York State's busiest waterway when the nation was a-building.

There were many well-known ships on the Great Lakes. Two that made history were the *Great Lakes Flyer* and the *Octavia*, a liner that carried many passengers and was later sold to become a Pacific transport. The sale was a fillip to shipbuilders on the Great Lakes, for it happened just as an eastern writer had commented of their industry: "Ships and their gear are like those in the East, but *cruder*."

At the head of the Erie Canal, Buffalo in the nineteenth century was a flourishing city (see Ill. 41). Grain from the Midwest came down the Lakes to Buffalo, to be transferred to canal boats and taken to New York, and from there to ports all over the world (see Ill. 42). The trade *from* New York was just as constant. There seemed to be a never-ending stream of emigrants for points

41. The harbor at Buffalo on Lake Erie—the take-off for points west, and the port where cargo was received from the lakes to be sent on east down the Erie Canal. *Ballou's Pictorial Drawing-Room Companion, 1850*

west. These were circumstances that helped to produce paintings and prints for the delight of collectors. The well-known George Catlin, visiting his brother in Lockport, made four prints of the Erie Canal that are highly sought collectors' items.

Charles Dickens in his *American Notes* gives an amusing and original impression of the early steamboats. On his trip from Pittsburgh to the Mississippi he described one:

> These western vessels are still more foreign to all the ideas we are accustomed to entertain of boats. In the first place they have no mast, cordage, tackle, rigging, or other such boat-like gear; nor have they anything in their shape at all calculated to remind one of a boat's head, stern, sides, or keel. Except that they are in the water and display a couple of paddle-like boxes, they might be intended for anything. . . .*

Anyone who saw "the great body of fire that rage[d] and roar[ed] beneath the frail pile of painted wood" found it easy to understand Dickens's wonder, "not that there should be so many fatal accidents, but that any journey should be safely made."

The craft that plied our inland waters were many and varied: steamers, flat-bottomed riverboats, schooners, dugout canoes, ferry boats, rafts—all quite

---

*Charles Dickens, *American Notes and the Uncommercial Traveler* (Boston: Estes and Lauriat, 1882; Cambridge edition), p. 190.

42. An old print showing grain boats leaving Chicago with wheat for the world. *America Illustrated*

43. Excursions on steamers were the great attraction on any river—such speed, such excitement—and of course they wouldn't blow up while *you* were on them. *Harper's Weekly*

different from the coastal shipping. My own interest began with a lake steamer, *Walk-in-the-Water*. She was the first to steam out on the Great Lakes, and as vivid to me as if I had walked her decks. Built in Black Rock, where I had often picnicked—a hamlet soon absorbed into the city of Buffalo—she had her picturesque name given to her by the Indians. I reveled in the fact that she an-nounced her arrival in port by shooting a small cannon—it seemed a fitting way for a ship called *Walk-in-the-Water* to enter a port! She predated me by about a century and a half. (The steam whistle had not been invented; hence, the use of the cannon.)

In the Northwest, the Columbia River played a vital role in opening the wilderness to settlement and trade. It was discovered in 1792 by Captain Robert Gray of Boston on his second journey to the West Coast in his ship *Columbia Rediviva*. Though navigators had been actively searching since the sixteenth century for a great river as a possible Northwest Passage, Gray's voyage to the Northwest Coast was for the purpose of engaging in the lucrative sea otter trade. In barter with the Northwest Indians, trade goods from New England were exchanged for luxurious sea otter pelts, and the pelts then traded in China for oriental goods, which were returned to New England for sale.

By 1792, many tribes had become shrewd in their dealings with the white traders, driving increasingly hard bargains. In addition, the sea otter population was being rapidly depleted. Thus traders were continually looking for virgin territory—any inlet or bay where trade might be carried on. Probably this, as much as dreams of the glory of discovery, was in Gray's mind when, on May 11, 1792, he sailed into "a large river of fresh water," which he proceeded to name Columbia. (As a sidelight on the vagaries of commerce, trade turned out to be poor in the river.)

44. On early steamers, smokestacks were such a status symbol! Even in the years after World War I, smokestacks retained their appeal. *Harper's Weekly, 1861*

45. A view of the forepart of a model of the *T. J. Potter,* which was a well-known steamboat in the Northwest, typical of the many that played such an important part in settling the country. *Columbia River Maritime Museum*

At the mouth of the river, J. J. Astor's Fur Trading Company established one of its scores of trading posts in 1811. That post today is Astoria, with the largest fishing fleet in the state, worn but dignified houses on its hills rising from the main street, and the Columbia River Maritime Museum, which dramatizes the region's nautical history in an outstanding collection.

Living today throughout the United States are descendants of the ship-masters whose acumen and daring made history, but few know them or the stories they have to tell of the clippers, the square-riggers, the schooners their forebears sailed on the high seas of long ago. Only a few treasure a sea chest, captain's desk, or sextant that made the journey to Canton and to San Francisco, to Liverpool and to the Persian Gulf. Yet their stories are our stories. Any sincere and honest collector can be the scribe, the instrument that makes it possible for these wisps of history to go to a marine museum or a local historical society, instead of being blown into obscurity by the winds of time.

Many surprising stories came to light as I looked for the physical reminders of an age that is past. Those were the days when a successful trip to the Orient could mean $300,000 or more to a ship's owners, and to the crew and its officers adventure, fear, labor, and ever-widening horizons. Certainly I never expected to find, in the quiet hills of western New York, nautical antiques from one of the most colorful and best known of the clippers, the *David Crockett.* Launched in October, 1853, from the yards of Greenman and Company, one of the great

Fig. 4. The clipper ship. *Drawing by Louisette Barrett*

shipbuilders in Mystic, Connecticut, she was a sturdy ship with the beautiful lines of the clipper, and the speed. The owners were Handy & Everett of New York. The *David Crockett* became famous for her nineteen-day passage from New York to Liverpool in 1856, an unheard-of speed at that time.

Though the memory of these glorious days remains, a hundred years and more have erased the knowledge of the homey things—the cargoes the ships carried, the china the captains brought home to their wives, the scrimshaw their sailors made. All these add color. *The Magazine Antiques* uses the term "pedigreed antiques" in referring to antiques whose original owners—and the descendants who also have been owners—are known.

Finding such mementoes of the *David Crockett* in the beautiful home of Persis Hall in the wooded hills of western New York was memorable. Her grandfather had sailed, at nineteen, with Captain Burgess on his last journey on the *David Crockett,* and he so often told her the story of that last tragic journey that she almost feels as though she had taken it herself. On the way home, off the coast of Argentina, a terrible storm damaged one of the masts. Fearing for the ship's safety, Burgess sent a sailor up the mast to see if he could repair it. Three sailors went up in succession. One after another was washed overboard. Then Burgess went, himself. To the horror of the crew, their captain was also washed into the sea.

Burgess left no will, and most of the household goods he cherished were dispersed. But his personal possessions were given by the family to Mrs. Hall. She has his sextant, his compasses, his dividers, and his dispatch box—this last item went with him on all his twenty-five voyages to New York and San Francisco, and back. She also has a number of other personal things: pictures of the two Burgess ships, the *David Crockett* and the *Challenge,* a painting of the old homestead, some of the Lowestoft that Burgess brought to his wife from a special journey to Hong Kong, some Japanese yarn work, even a few pieces of scrimshaw made by sailors on his ship.

Something of the importance of the *David Crockett* in her day can be judged by the fact that she is claimed by two ports: San Francisco, where she was a familiar sight after her first arrival in July, 1857, and Mystic, where she

46. The figurehead of the *David Crockett* as portrayed by Jacob Anderson, an outstanding carver of New York City. The sturdy pioneer is shown in a deerskin suit, his rifle firmly clasped, his long hair flying free under his cap. His was a revered figure in the clipper ship era. *San Francisco Maritime Museum*

47. Blocks out of the attic of the old Burgess homestead in Somerset, Massachusetts. The story goes that Captain Burgess had planned to use them on that fabulous ship the *David Crockett,* which never needed repairs. But Burgess was washed overboard in a storm off Argentina. Three men, who had gone aloft to deal with a broken mast, were blown overboard first, so the captain himself went aloft and was also blown into the stormy seas. A hundred and some years later, the blocks remain but the *David Crockett* is gone, surviving only in the memory of those who love nautical lore. *Persis Pettis Hall Collection*

48. Persis Hall, whose grandfather as a boy of nineteen sailed with John Burgess on that last fatal journey around the Horn, owns what the family has always called "the dispatch box," the box with which he "ran the ship." In it went the captain's orders. An old seaman felt it must be the watch box, within which the ship's log was always put, but Mrs. Hall insists it came down in the family as "the dispatch box." *Persis Pettis Hall Collection*

was launched. For fifty years she sailed, bringing fortunes to her happy owners. Only once in all that time was she overhauled for repairs. She bowed to retirement in 1890, but continued in use as a barge in the Boston area.

One of the indirect joys of collecting nautical antiques is that you can always find previously untold stories of ships of the past. When I was staying at the Whaler's Inn in Mystic, I talked with its owner. She told me of her father, who had brought *half* a ship down the Erie Canal. The vessel had been ordered built in Buffalo for service in the Spanish-American War. When she was launched they discovered that she was too wide to make the trip to New York by way of the canal. Undaunted, the builders had her cut in half and her sides boarded up, and each half was taken down the canal. Their only miscalculation was their timetable. By the time the two halves reached New York and were welded together again, the war was over!

Sometimes it seems that it's the stories that make the antiques. You might try looking about in your own town for old seamen, or relatives who knew them well. It's a gaily colored path with many kinks. Things of the mind may well become your "best antiques."

49. The octant of Captain Burgess from the *David Crockett. Persis Pettis Hall Collection*

50. In twenty-five voyages from New York around the Horn to San Francisco, this compass never failed to bring the *David Crockett* home. *Persis Pettis Hall Collection*

3

SHIPS FOR THE
COLLECTOR

SHIP MODELS

MODELS OF VESSELS HAVE INTRIGUED Presidents and schoolboys. Their history stretches far back in time. One of the finest was found in the tomb of Tutankhamen; among interesting archeological finds in Jutland were models of ships that dated back to 1200 B.C.

Models have been made by many for quite different reasons. Some authorities believe that shipbuilding models, complete in every detail, were built one step ahead of the actual ship. Several early paintings picture the master shipbuilder explaining to a group around a table the details of the model before him. Until the latter part of the nineteenth century, few workers in a shipyard understood technical drawings; they had to build a ship from a model. If there are papers to prove it, and sometimes there are, ship models of this kind are among the most valuable of all. Richard Orcutt, a recognized sculptor in wood who grew up in the shipyards of Maine, had just such a model. Though his research did not furnish proof, the size of his model, its accuracy of detail, and perfect resemblance to a fishing schooner led him to believe that it was indeed a working model.

Over the centuries, ship models have been made as burial gifts to the dead, as votive offerings for churches, as showpieces of a goldsmith's skill, by sailors of their own ships, by marine artists as models for their paintings, and of course by builders of ships, by officers, architects, and a long list of talented and not so talented amateurs.

51. The most valuable and difficult models to find are those with papers—that is, models you can identify as made of a specific vessel and made to scale. This one of the American clipper *Swordfish* was made by A. Frazer with a scale of 3/32 of an inch equal to one foot. *South Street Seaport Museum*

52. Museums protect their best models with glass cases, just as the sailors did. The *Edward B. Winslow,* a large schooner displayed at the Bath Marine Museum, shows attention to detail in the furled sails, knots to secure the rigging, and the turned rail.

When my son was in the fifth and sixth grades, he spent most of his afternoons and evenings ignoring homework and building ship models of balsa wood. It was my introduction to the fascination of nautical objects—even those made by a child from commercial kits. Finally, my husband persuaded him to use the skill he had unconsciously been acquiring in the last several years to now construct a good plank model, carefully rigged. It took more than a year for him to complete it and enclose it in a glass case. Today, it is one of the decorative assets of his studio.

Erwin O. Christensen points out, in the *Index of American Design,* that in early America people whittled as commonly as today we doodle while we talk on the telephone. Many early ship models were whittled by sailors who loved them, and some show great professional competence; yet few have survived.

Should you come upon such a ship model, treat it with care; not many are to be found and masterpieces were sometimes created with a jackknife. One seaman wrote to his wife: "I have whittled a ship and a lighthouse for you with a pilot boat putting out to sea. It is a copy of the A. C. Watson, but you may give it a different name if you wish. She is a sweet little schooner." *

One cannot be interested in nautical antiques long without wanting a model of one's own. If you become a buyer, here are several facts to keep in mind. Models fall into two broad classifications—those that are built to scale, and those that are purely decorative and not built to scale. A collector's prize is a model that has been built to scale. Take, for instance, the *Mayflower*. It has always been a popular model, but it has always been considered a decorative model rather than one made to scale. An article in the *Christian Science Monitor* of January 17, 1971, described the efforts of two English marine architects, Bill Ward and David McGregor, to change this. Through research, they uncovered enough details to make possible an accurate model of the most famous ship in our history.

---

* New Brunswick Historical Society. Collection #16, 1861. "Letters of a Cheney Settlement Sailor," E. A. Baird, p. 125.

53. Modern models have pressed parts, and sometimes the smaller pieces are machine-cut. Often an old model has been painted and repainted to preserve it, and then the layers of paint are an indication of age. This model at the Rhode Island Historical Society represents the schooner *R. W. Cornstock* and dates from the end of the nineteenth century.

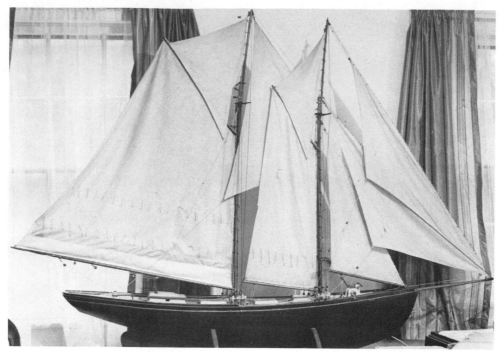

54. Some old models may be quite crude. The sailor who made them may have had inadequate tools, perhaps just his knife. The neater the job, the more accurate the presentation, the prouder you will be of the model. This one is nearly five feet long, quite a feat of workmanship. *Orcutt Collection*

Models of the *Santa Maria* and other early craft are usually described by nautical experts as "conjectural models." They are "conjectural" only because the plans for the original vessel are not extant. The model builder may have had, on the other hand, excellent and detailed plans based on conjecture. Thus, conjectural models are often built to scale and can be extremely valuable.

Models built in modern times representing old vessels are valuable if they have been well researched. Fifty years ago a high school student, Albert M. MacCleary, made a name for himself by carefully researching the background of the clipper ship *The Flying Cloud,* which has always been popular with model makers and collectors. MacCleary not only captured the feeling of this famous and colorful ship; he built it accurately to scale. It became a very valuable model.

The Francis Russell Hart Nautical Museum in Cambridge, Massachusetts, has a fine display of nautical items under the jurisdiction of the Massachusetts Institute of Technology's Department of Ocean Engineering. More than seventy models can be seen, ranging from early sailing ships to modern merchant vessels. Working drawings are available, and these are invaluable to the maker of true-to-scale-and-detail models.

The fact that two Presidents, Franklin D. Roosevelt and John F. Kennedy, were extremely fond of ship models has, of course, added to public interest. President Kennedy's collection of ship models is on display at the United States Navy Memorial Museum in Washington, D.C. Those belonging to President

55. Sometimes one aspect of a model sets it apart. This one has cabins and hatches made of bone. *Ellen Fales Lomasney*

56. Model of the U. S. frigate *Constitution* rigged as she was rigged in 1861. It was for sale at the South Street Seaport Museum shop. A vessel with the original rigging has more value than one that has been re-rigged.

57. Masts on schooners increased from two to seven as cargoes grew in bulk in the last half of the nineteenth century. The four-master, however, proved very practical. Models of schooners with more than two masts as well done as this one at the Bath Marine Museum do not turn up often.

58. When sailing vessels were finally ousted by steam, the craftsmen who constructed models turned to the more modern vessels. It is most unusual to find a model of a steamship with the square-rigging that conservative shipbuilders clung to long after steam had proved its worth. *Photograph by Bern C. Ritchie & Co.*

59. Quite out of the ordinary is this little tug at the Columbia River Maritime Museum. Tugs were hardworking vessels in the new age of steam. For years even the schooners were dependent on tugs to tow them upstream and in and out of harbors.

Roosevelt are in the Roosevelt Library at Hyde Park. Frigates, sloops of war, and clipper ships were Roosevelt's special love, though his collection of models ranges from Chinese junks to submarines.

If you have found a model that you like, here are some points to check. If the model does not measure up, wait; you will certainly find one that does.

1. The rigging is important. Look it over carefully. Few who do not thoroughly understand a sailing vessel's complicated network of spars and rigging can rig a model properly. It's a time-consuming job, even if you know how to do it. With President Roosevelt, it was a labor of love. He rerigged several of his vessels. Good rigging usually means a good model.

2. Be sure there are no pressed parts. They take a ship out of the good model class. Parts must be whittled or carved by hand.

3. Don't pass up a model because you can see that it has been repainted several times. Many connoisseurs consider this a mark of genuineness.

4. Keep in mind the ideal. You want a model with good details, with tiny rope ladders, carved dinghies, tall symmetrical masts, well-planed decks.

5. A model of special interest is one carved in bas-relief. Many men who worked on sailing vessels carved out schooners and clippers in bas-relief in their later years, in retirement.

The cost of ship models, as researched recently in a very elaborate marine antiques store, was from $150 to $3,260. Immediately one asks, "What made the difference?" The highest-priced one was a prisoner of war model of H.M.S.

60. A steamboat model is a rare find, particularly one as carefully done as this one from the Columbia River Maritime Museum.

61. A quite different model on display at the Columbia River Maritime Museum. The lines are sleek and modern—yet something of the old form is still there.

62. Models of naval vessels such as the U.S.S. *Oregon*, displayed at the Columbia River Maritime Museum, were not made so often as square-riggers and other sailing vessels. The *Oregon* is probably owned by more citizens in this country than any other dismantled vessel. She was sold for 19¢ a pound to anyone who wanted any part of her—and her parts thus achieved wide distribution as future nautical antiques.

Ceres, in tortoiseshell and ivory. Such models are rare; most of them are in museums. You can be sure, if you come upon one made of these materials, and with fine details, that you are indeed one in a thousand or more. The term "prisoner of war model" is applied to fine work, usually done in bone, evidencing hours of careful, painstaking effort, with a fine show of detail that alone makes them distinctive (see Ill. 66). Most are in cases (this one was), and these are also important. Cases not only protect the model, but quietly say, "This is quality."

63. If you seek for quality in your models, study those in the best nautical museums for examples. This one is the rigged model of the four-masted iron bark *Kenilworth,* built by Carroll Ray Sawyer, ca. 1930. *Mystic Seaport photograph, Mystic, Connecticut. Photograph by Lester D. Olin*

64. The rigging of a model is one gauge of quality. Note how it is done and the thread used for it. The top model here is the brig *Independence;* the other is a Baltimore clipper, the *Wasp* —at the Columbia River Maritime Museum.

65. Models with sails are found less frequently. They have a somewhat different quality. As with all models, however, the detail and rigging should be accurate. *Old Toll House Antiques*

66. This particular prisoner of war model is unusual on many counts. First, simply because it *is* a prisoner of war model. Modern P.O.W.s speak of the importance to their survival of the opportunity to do creative handicraft. This model is also unusual because it is made of split beef bones, a difficult material to work with. In addition, the original case has survived, which is rare. This case has a mirror-back, something sailors in all countries liked to use to enhance their work. The model is also early—dating between about 1793 and 1815. *Photograph by Bern C. Ritchie & Co.*

SCRIMSHAW AND BONE MODELS

Models of vessels in bone are the aristocrats of ship models, even though they are largely decorative and not made to scale. Most of the scrimshaw models were the work of crewmen on whaling vessels. Many of the finest bone models are prisoner of war models. The materials were cheap, but long hours of boredom were healed by the handiwork that has created masterpieces for us to admire.

Scrimshaw models often combine whalebone, popularly referred to as whale ivory, or true whale ivory—the whale's teeth—with wood. The beauty of the wood, the manner in which it is used in the planking, and other details put these models too in the art classification. As with any work of art, the value rises with the skill of the worker, his knowledge of his subject, and the artistry of his presentation.

In an auction recently of rare whaling and marine items, a featured model was a scrimshaw one of a whaleship. It was made entirely of whalebone, rigged with a cutting stage. A piece of baleen even simulated a blanket piece of blubber being taken in over the side. Such originality of execution—showing blubber being brought in, for example—adds immensely to the value of any model.

There were times when sailors availed themselves of other bones, such as beef bone, for scrimshaw work. Of course, with scrimshaw models as with others, sometimes one comes upon a bargain. The best I have heard of was a miniature scrimshaw model six inches long that a friend of mine bought for fifty dollars. Perhaps if you search, after careful study, you too will find a sleeper. Usually, however, you rejoice at just finding such a model at any price, for they are rare. Nonetheless, at a New York antiques show not long ago, three scrimshaw models of ships were displayed for sale. The prices were in the thousands.

HALF-MODELS

To hold a half-model in one's hand is to hold a portion of the sailing history of our country. From such were the sailing ships of the United States built—frigates, schooners, privateers, fishing craft, and the more glamorous clippers and yachts.

From the time of the Revolution until about 1850, designers and builders of ships worked entirely with half-models. Then, gradually, it became the practice to draw ship plans first on paper, superseding the use of half-models except as a building aid. But pure science was long in taking over. Half-models were used in many a shipbuilding yard far into the twentieth century.

Naval architects laid out these half-hulls with great care. Usually the hull was in laminated sections, which served as a pattern for the vessel. In rare instances, the half-hull was designed with the wooden framing showing. Half-hulls for smaller vessels were occasionally carved out in bas-relief.

67. Half-models of earlier ships were frequently made by carvers. This one illustrates the galleons of the seventeenth and eighteenth centuries.

68. You can learn to recognize half-models by their lines. This one of the *Chrysopolis* at the San Francisco Maritime Museum has the long, easily distinguished lines of a riverboat.

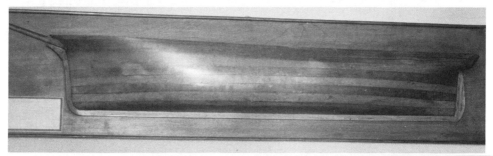

69. The fine lines of the clipper, tapered at the bow for speed, are apparent on this model at the San Francisco Maritime Museum.

70. The barkentine, sturdy but lacking the sleekness of the clipper's lines. Note the large capacity of the hull. This half-model of the *Amaranth* is on display at the San Francisco Maritime Museum.

If you find one, you cannot mistake it, though my son puzzled over two carved bulges he found on each side of the fireplace in a house he bought (see Ill. 71). They were half-hulls mounted upside down. Usually half-hulls are mounted on a board; often the masts are indicated. You will find them hanging on the walls of all marine museums. They vary somewhat in size, but they were all built carefully to scale. For the larger vessels, a scale of one-eighth of an inch to one foot was used. A larger scale was used with smaller vessels.

Half-model is the term of the collector. To the ship owner, the naval architect, the builder, it was a builder's model or the lift model. Now that ships are no longer built from such models, half-model is the term generally used in referring to them.

The half-model is the joy of all boat owners. Many long to have one of the ship they love. Many have one carved, but that is *after* their boat has been built. Because interest in half-hulls has become so great, numerous marine museums are selling replicas, just as art museums have reproductions of some of their treasures reproduced.

It is believed that the use of these models for building ships was discovered quite by accident in 1790. The *Eliza*, which is preserved in the Peabody Museum in Salem, is the earliest known model of this type. Built by Enos Briggs of Salem, the *Eliza* was launched in June of 1794 or 1795.

Orlando Merrill, the designer of the sloop *Wasp*, which figured so prominently in the War of 1812, is given credit in many books for the discovery. Actually, the *Wasp* was launched after the *Eliza*. Some authorities believe the reason Merrill was given the credit was that he so greatly improved the method, doweling the laminated parts together, and making it much easier for the builder to transfer the model plans to paper and to the actual building of the ship. Others believe that, although these two builders' models are the earliest known, the principle may have been developed still earlier, but the makers of these two vessels got the credit.

There is no doubt that the United States was the first to use this type of builder's model. European models were of the skeleton type. When the use of half-models was initiated here, shipbuilding procedures changed enormously, for it became possible to follow the design of the naval architect accurately. Because the parts were doweled together, they could be taken apart—and the sheer, body, and half-breadth plan could be transferred to paper. These are the three important plans necessary to build a ship. In the days when the designer of a vessel depended upon his eye alone, this discovery stood as a monumental one in naval history.

The model was sent to the building loft. There its lines were taken off, one section at a time. Two flat rulers were used, one placed dead against the keel, the other perpendicular. The lines from the half-model, scaled to the exact size of the ship, were transferred to the mold loft floor, using chalk. Thin pieces of wood were laid out along the chalk lines and tacked together. The templates thus made were used as patterns in shaping the ship's timbers, which were *not* transferred to the mold loft.

Some ship owners treasured these models jealously. The daughter of the founder and owner of one of the great shipbuilding companies in Bath, Maine, has a house filled with treasures from the days when her father's name was known wherever sailing vessels went, but she has not a single half-model of any ship her father built. However, there was a beautiful half-model on her wall.

She remembered the day she asked her father for a half-model of her own. Though the walls of his office were covered with half-models of vessels that had slid down the ways in his shipyard, each one had too much meaning to him, to part with it—even to his daughter. Instead, he sent her to the attic to find one there, and the one she chose is now on her wall.

Good half-models were top secrets in the shipping circles of those days. Every builder was interested in the model of rival yards, hoping it might bring him a new idea that would make his ships better. The Sewells were master shipbuilders. Mr. A. Sewell had his master model, and though it was interpreted somewhat differently in different vessels built in the yard, there was always enough of the distinctive Sewell flair so that a vessel could be recognized as Sewell built. That indescribable sheer meant more to the initiated than the Sewell flag that flew with the Stars and Stripes.

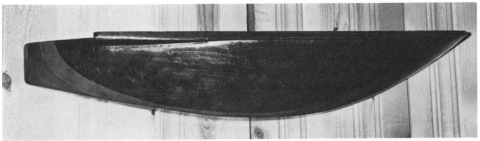

71. A nineteenth-century schooner half-model made of mahogany and pine. The sections can be taken apart by removing two screws in the back. This half-model was once part of a mantel in a Connecticut home.

72. Half-model of a three-masted cargo schooner. It was not carved to be taken apart for measurements. You can sometimes tell whether a half-model is for a square-rigger or a schooner by the placement of the masts. The draft is less on a schooner so that it can maneuver in the shallow harbors and rivers along the coast.

73. A shipbuilder commissions a master craftsman to design and carve a half-hull, or half-model, which becomes a three-dimensional plan for his vessel. "What do you want *half* a boat for?" a friend asked me. To those who know, a half-model is one of the most desirable of nautical antiques. This one at the Columbia River Maritime Museum has a graceful sheer—the topmost line that runs from stem to stern. The sections, known as lifts, indicate an especially good model.

Half-models are very reliable indicators of the ships of their day, except in the case of clippers and yachts. In both these instances speed was the element that made the vessels great, and sometimes traps were laid to confuse rival builders. As an example of an occasional variance between a designer's model and

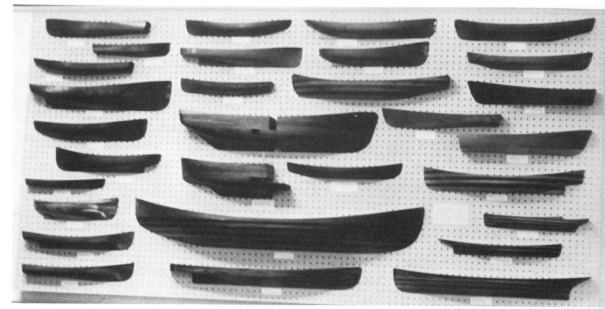

74. One of the best ways to learn to distinguish half-models is to study them in museums. This display at the Columbia River Maritime Museum shows models designed by boatbuilders around Astoria, Oregon. It includes vessels from tugboats and launches to gillnetters and trawlers. A rare model is the partially separated one in the center; its bow section can be built either with a purse seiner stern (as displayed) or with a troller stern, as shown below it.

the vessel as built, there was some slight doubt in identifying the model of the *America,* although the New York Yacht Club has kept every half-model of its ships. George Steers, who designed the *America,* made changes in the design before she was built. As the templates lay on the loft floor, the master builder changed a line here and a line there. When complete, she was not an exact replica of the half-model. This schooner, which gave her name to the cup for which many would race in the years to come, does not have an exact model of her own.

Builders of clipper ships, where speed meant fame and greater profits, were likewise "protective" of their models.

Half-models were formerly very common. Stories are told of using them for firewood in Maine. There were so many about of the lesser ships that no one could possibly have foreseen a half-model would become valuable. Only a few years ago an antiques dealer in Nova Scotia had an attic full of these models, which she sold to tourists for a fairly modest sum. My neighbor bought a three-masted schooner, which I greatly admired. When he went back a year later to buy another, the dealer had none left. "A man from New York bought them all," she told him. "I've always been able to pick them up, so I sold them— expecting to replenish my stock during the winter. But they were all gone. I

Fig. 5. The *America. Drawing*
by Louisette Barrett

THE AMERICA

only found two or three half-models; they used to be everywhere."

Most collectors set the date of 1960 as the time when half-models began to disappear. At that time many marine museums were being built, and marine artifacts became more valuable. Half-models that are authentic can still be found, however. They just cost more.

Once you have found a half-model, you will want to identify it as closely as you can. It is not likely that you will be able to tell what ship was built from it, but you can find out what type of ship it was. To the novice all models look alike, yet there are such differences in their lines that experts can immediately tell the general type.

Howard I. Chapelle, a well-known authority on naval craft, estimates that between 1800 and 1900 there were more than a hundred types of American sailing craft. But to the boys who shipped to sea at twelve, as to the men who worked in shipyards building these vessels, ships were as distinctive as different automobiles are to boys today. They could tell in what shipbuilding yard a craft was made, and who its designers were. And the captains of the sailing vessels could tell at a glance whose ship they passed or raced on their voyages. In Hong Kong, San Francisco, Boston, Liverpool—and in Maine—they met and talked of the shipping world and of their vessels.

Half-models were designed for making individual ships. Often, only two were built from the same half-model; the largest number was ten. Albert Winslow, who was designing ships from 1860 to 1895, was famous both for his ships' designs and for his "eye." He designed the largest two-master, the largest three-

75. A model of the *L.C.M.,* out of Newbury, Massachusetts, complete to the tiniest detail. It has a real compass, sliding hatch covers, running lights, and even rope coils. The engine also is built to scale. Even more unusual, there is a half-model besides. Both were offered for sale at a New York antiques show. *The Herald Corbins*

master, and the first four-masted schooner designed as such. It took him from two to five weeks to carve a model. Great as were the ships he turned out, he received only a hundred dollars for a model. A large number of his models are preserved in Taunton, Massachusetts.

Possibly Donald McKay was the greatest designer of them all. His designing of clipper ships brought him worldwide fame. When his ships made their breathtaking journeys to Liverpool, San Francisco, and the Orient, the shipbuilding

76. For those who have a special interest in the vessels of a certain builder, or trace their family history to perhaps a former mate or captain, it is exciting to find both a half-model and a drawing of the same schooner. The half-model of the *Eleanor A. Percy* is displayed at the Bath Marine Museum. It is laminated, which gives it a special beauty as well as utility for the builder. And it is identified, something that is unusual among models. Too many went into kindling for the fire, much the way some eighteenth-century furniture did.

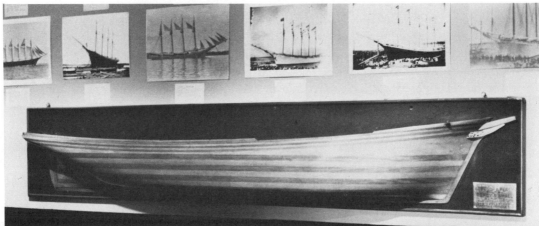

77. A pen-and-ink drawing of the schooner shown in the preceding illustration.

world was astounded. Even today his name is mentioned with reverence and respect as one of the great practitioners of naval architecture. How fortunate one would be to find a half-model of one of his ships!

On many a half-model the placement of the masts was indicated, but on others it was not. To identify the latter may take research. The easiest method is to get the opinion of an old seaman. Lacking that opportunity, you must turn to books.

Identifying the source of some half-models, or even what type of ship they served to build, sometimes seems an almost impossible task for the collector. You may be content just to possess an old model to hang on the wall. However, several books have been published giving plans of old vessels, and by carefully comparing your half-model with the sheer plan given on these vessels, you may discover the type of half-model yours is. Whatever it is, it can lead you into a greater knowledge of ships and of a world that is gone.

SHIPS IN BOTTLES

Few ships in bottles have survived, yet these intricate miniatures so painstakingly constructed by sailors must, according to some authorities, have been almost a commonplace in a sailor's whittling life. The very wonder of a full-rigged ship model encased in such a small space makes ships in bottles a collector's delight. They are indeed excellent examples of careful work—work undertaken to make sure the product of the long hours of craftsmanship would withstand the rigors of the voyage home.

Precarious protection the bottles were, it has turned out, for few have come down to us. But it is only in this century that full measure of appreciation

AMERICAN NAUTICAL ART AND ANTIQUES

for this type of craftsmanship has been reached. Naturally, the scarcity of authentic examples, plus the growing desire of collectors, has resulted in the making of reproductions. Large numbers of ships in bubbly green glass were manufactured in England in the 1940s. Many are available for sale—full-rigged ships in green bottles, quaint and interesting—so it is important to be able to distinguish between a commercially made model and one made by a crewman of a long-gone ship.

The fact that the little ship in the bottle is an actual replica of the one in which the craftsman sailed adds historical value to its charm. That lone little model may be the only memento of the sturdy craft that battled wind and sea and adversity as a speck in an ocean of immensity.

A rule of thumb that helps in recognizing age and authenticity is to compare the size of ship and bottle—the larger the ship in relation to its enclosure, the better the piece (see Ill. 79). Still, there are some delicate old models in which this rule does not hold. The next criterion in identification is the quality of the materials used. Bone and mahogany were employed for some excellent small models, which often are in bottles that are big for the ship's size.

Both standing and running rigging must be correct in every detail in these small models. Running rigging is the movable rope used to brace yards and to make, or take in, sail. Standing rigging largely supports the masts. Unfortunately, many collectors have little experience in this intricate subject—ropes are ropes, and that is that. However, a novice can learn. Actual experience with sail is a great teacher. Without that, an intimate study of ships and their rigging, where the rigging shows, can change one's viewpoint. You will not be satisfied with a few pieces of twine draped about a mast.

A beautiful sheer—the curve of a ship's deck between bow and stern—is

78. The patience and skill it took for a seaman to manipulate a ship into a bottle make these models now one of the most popular of nautical antiques. Even these days, when reproductions abound to supply the demand, the best ones show good craftsmanship. Ships in bottles were really a seaman's craft; the bottle was necessary to protect the sailor's delicate work. Although such models give ample evidence of the effort that went into them, an early lack of appreciation led to the old ones becoming scarce, hence expensive, today. *Nina Hellman Antiques*

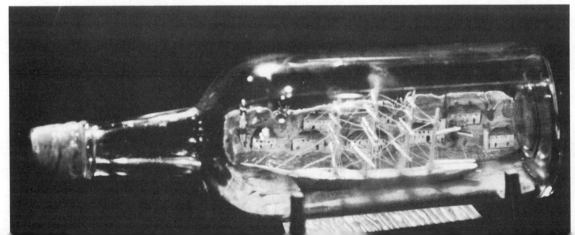

79. You can tell if a model is old rather than new. Study the detail of the vessel. The smaller the bottle in proportion to the size of the ship, the better. And a narrow neck on a large bottle indicates greater skill by the builder. Check the age of the bottle. Bubbly glass has been made a long time, but it is a good indication of age. If the glass is clear (although it has some bubbles) and the bottle has a bulbous shape like this one from The Mariners Museum in Newport News, it is especially good.

also important. Study the examples in marine museums—you may find yourself exclaiming, like the connoisseur you've become, "What a beautiful sheer!"

To make the sails of their model ships in bottles, sailors used paper, cloth, or thin wood carved and painted. Most of the hulls were whittled from wood. The yards, often made from the thick matches in use at the time, are a helpful point in identifying a really old ship-in-bottle.

In making the model, the workman folded up the rigging, umbrella fashion, laid the masts and sails flat with the decks, each one attached to a gov-

80. A ship with the sails down, strings attached for pulling them up, is inserted in the narrow neck of a bottle en route to its position inside. Then the strings will be pulled, the sails will flutter into place, and the bottle can be sealed. In this display at the San Francisco Maritime Museum, the model at the right has the necessary strings attached. In the neck of the bottle at the left can be seen a model with the sails down, in the process of being inserted. (Note the ropework wine glass in the foreground.)

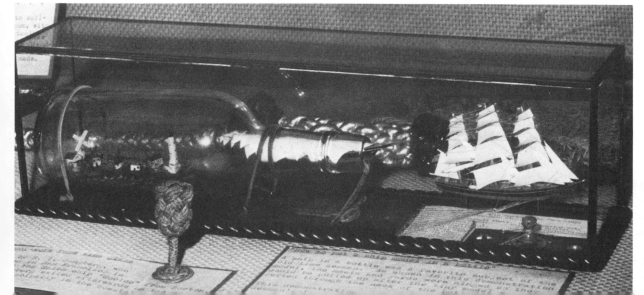

erning string. When all was complete, the big moment came: the model was slipped into the bottle, which often had been prepared with elaborate scenery— a sea, a lighthouse, or a tug as background interest. The strings were pulled, and sails and masts sprang upright (see Ill. 80). The governing rope was then either sheared off or tucked into the sea to serve as anchor rope.

Although, when set beside some well-done reproductions, the original sailor's model may seem clumsy, it is still by far the better choice for a collection. A ship in a bottle made by a true present-day cratfsman is next best to one made a hundred years ago. If lovingly done, it will prove to be the antique of the future. The commercial model never will achieve that stature.

SHADOW BOXES

Waterline models and shadow boxes are elusive if pursued through the pages of reference books, but not wholly so in "real life," as it were. Ask a dealer, particularly one in an East Coast shop, if he has a good shadow box model, and likely as not he will go to a shelf and produce one.

Shadow box is the term for the frame constructed by the sailor-craftsman for displaying and preserving his precious waterline model. These models, as the name implies, show the vessel as it rides the waves when a good part of the hull is covered. Some are complete ship replicas from the water up, but the greater number are half a ship. Often a mirror has been placed at the back of the case to convey an illusion of a full rounded ship in motion. A painting of the sea, or a lighthouse, may add to the artistry.

81. Ships in shadow boxes were sometimes referred to as waterline models because the hull below the waterline is covered by waves. A large number of these models were made by sailors, who were most accustomed to seeing their vessels in the water. The rigging on these is usually excellent because the sailor-craftsman knew the lines well. Some shadow boxes have a mirror behind the ship to make it appear a whole ship instead of half a hull. Usually the boxes are shallow and framed with glass in front. The waves were made of various substances: putty, shavings, even carved wood. This shadow box is at the Columbia River Maritime Museum.

82. This two-masted schooner in a shadow box stands as a reminder of the days when the two-master plied the coast carrying everything from passengers to hay and wood from town to town. In those times, travel and commerce took advantage of the only good highways the nation had—the sea lanes. *Nina Hellman Antiques*

83. It is not difficult to tell that this model was made by a seaman. It is of the *Thomas W. Lawson,* the only seven-masted schooner ever built. When viewed through the glass cover, it appears professional enough, but with the glass removed (as here), you can see how the maker had to cut away a part of the case to make room for the last sail. He also had to cut a hole in the other end of the case for the bowsprit.

The models were mounted on board, and the board decorated to simulate the sea. The waves were made of putty or shavings (many a sailor was a better craftsman with his knife than with his brush). Before folk art came to be appreciated, these were more or less unsung works of art, but today they are greatly valued. In a shop where most prices were fairly modest, I saw a shadow box model priced at two hundred dollars.

Because they are sailors' work, interest in shadow boxes is rising. Sailors knew their ships, and in their waterline models accuracy in details, in rigging, is almost guaranteed. It is not a "made up" ship you will be hanging on your wall.

The boxes are not deep—from three to five and one-half inches, with the narrower depths predominating. The sails are often made of wood and skillfully bellied out in carving so that the ship appears to be sailing before the wind. Or they may be compressed to fit into the box. You will also find sails made of paper, but properly rigged.

The craftsman often embellished his frame fittingly with gold leaf and designs to properly complement a work of love. Of course, many waterline models were merely mounted on a plank, but fewer of these have been preserved.

84. The ideal is a collage well-painted, the ship with thin wooden sails, pure lines on the hull, all tied together in a scene. *Orcutt Collection*

4

SCULPTURES OF THE SEA

NOTABLE SHIP CARVINGS

ONE OF THE MOST TANGIBLE of arts—the carving on early ships—lives on chiefly in written descriptions. Time and the sea have all but obliterated the many carvings that graced the ships of the American Colonies and those of Europe in the seventeenth and eighteenth centuries. It was the custom of those times to paint, to gild, to carve, not only the prow of a vessel but the stern and most of the area between. Even the unlikely and unpoetic guns were wreathed in elaborate carvings of acanthus leaves, vines, and flowers—and adorned, perhaps more appropriately, with victory crowns.

This carving was so massive that in some instances it actually interfered with the mobility of the ship. One captain, it is said, sawed off the carvings on which so much time, skill, and money had been lavished, once he got out to sea. Obviously, he was a man more interested in maneuvering his ship than in art for the winds and waves.

A Viking ship unearthed near Oslo was covered with carvings. It is preserved for our delight and appreciation through a superstition that dictated the actual burying of ships. The *Vasa,* royal ship of King Gustav of Sweden, was recently raised from a more suitable watery grave in the Baltic. Restoration revealed more than seventy-five separate carvings.

In the late eighteenth century the French, who had made some of the most beautiful ship carvings, realized that the decorations were exceeding the vessels themselves in value, and they began putting an end to the practice of adorning their ships in this way. While the art flourished, however, it produced a carver in every port. Not all were accomplished sculptors, but many could carve, and

67

everyone could whittle. If all these masterpieces could have come to rest in dry dock, what a heritage would be ours!

A growing interest in the ship's speed and utility replaced this early artistic preoccupation. Sterns ceased to resemble elaborately decorated three-story buildings. Five dragons or a group of lions on the prow dwindled to one.

A collector can hardly hope to find a ship carving that dates before the nineteenth century. Yet sometimes, in tantalizing abandon, Neptune himself digs deep in the sands of time and drops such a treasure carelessly on shore. For instance, a figurehead thought by scholars to have graced a Roman ship was washed up on the shores of Tunisia. And the Peabody Museum in Salem owns the head of a woman, elaborately carved and crowned, part of a figurehead found floating in the Atlantic.

An idea of the popularity of ship carving is found in the list of men engaged in the craft compiled by Pauline A. Pinckney in her book, *American Figureheads and Their Carvers.** Collected from newspaper accounts, directories in coastal cities, family papers, and navy records, the list covers eighteen pages of fine print. The author endeavored to include only carvers for ships, but the task was difficult—many carvers turned to any task at hand in slack times of ship carving.

Because so little of the work remains for critical judgment, it is hard to name the greatest carvers of the past. One of them was certainly William Rush of Philadelphia (see Ill. 85), who was a prolific letter writer as well as a prolific carver. His influence spread far because of his apprentice system and his close association with Joshua Humphrey of the United States Navy. He taught many the art of ship carving, and encouraged others up and down the Atlantic seaboard, as well as recommending them for commissions. Through his efforts, in those days when travel was difficult, a feeling of unity of interest was nurtured among the carvers in all the important ports.

Wood carvings offer a wide-open field for collectors. You may not find that rare prize, a figurehead, but other beautiful pieces are waiting for discovery and use. Enterprising men have bought and saved parts of old ships that were being broken up. Hatch covers were often carved, and they make fine tables. Pieces of the *Queen Mary* and *Normandie* are stored in warehouses, to be made into collectible furnishings for American homes.

Many an old carving languishes in an out-of-the-way antiques shop, awaiting the collector of nautical antiques. You may find a masterpiece, but the time to act is now. Nautical treasures are being sought out, from Vancouver, British Columbia, to San Diego, California; from Nova Scotia to Florida. A modest investment today can mean much tomorrow, and in many places tomorrow has already come.

---

* W. W. Norton & Company, New York, 1940.

85. William Rush, from a painting by Peale. Rush of Philadelphia was not only a great carver, but the moving spirit back of much of the ship carving in the early days of our nation. He taught the art to many young men; he wrote to carvers up and down the coast, kept in touch with them, recommended them for commissions to carve. Carving was his love, and he made it truly the sculpture of the sea. *Courtesy of National Historic Park*

86. This is the bow ornament, cast from metal, of the U.S.S. *Des Moines,* a turn-of-the-century navy cruiser, on display at the Columbia River Maritime Museum.

FIGUREHEADS

For centuries, carvings have been an intrinsic part of a ship. Lingering longest into the present is the figurehead, a mystic symbol for seafaring men, a highly sought treasure for collectors. The figurehead combines something of a votive offering to the angry gods of the sea with the helpful presence of a guardian angel of the ship. Quite unseen by the carver, myths, superstitions, and religious beliefs entered into its makeup. Sailors have risked their lives to save a figurehead from a stranded vessel. When a ship is dismantled, the figurehead lives on, preserved with reverence—by the captain, the owner, or some fortunate person who has succeeded in laying claim to it.

Figureheads are the finest of early American wood carvings. They were the crowning luxury of our sailing ships from the time of the Colonies to the early part of the twentieth century. No one knows when they were first used. Some authorities surmise that primitive man, his head covered to represent an animal and thus scare off the enemy, may have been a source of the conception. Hawaiian canoes sometimes carried skulls as warning figureheads. The fierce lions used as figureheads on European ships had a similar connotation. Leif Ericson and his men were under orders not to take into Icelandic waters boats having hideous heads, "for the natives were so superstitious they would feel they were embodied sea monsters and would run and hide."

Records turned up in nautical research indicate the use of figureheads on Egyptian ships in the second century B.C. and on Roman ships in A.D. 50. Great interest is attached to the fact that, in the story of Paul's journey from Malta to Syracuse, the ship was adorned with a figurehead of Castor and Pollux. James Moffatt, in his biblical translation, speaks of the ship with "the Dioscuri as figureheads."

Figureheads were copied and recopied in the seventeenth and eighteenth centuries, and so today it is difficult to determine where a figurehead was originally carved, on what vessel it sailed, or who made it. English ships of war bore the royal lion. To the Europeans, the Indian was the symbol of the American colonies. William Rush was noted for his Indian carvings.

Describing his figurehead for the frigate *United States,* Rush wrote: "As the United States is to be the Great Empire of Liberty, it should be represented by the Goddess of Liberty, supported by the American arms, Peace, Commerce, Agriculture." When completed, her head was crowned with a crest adorned with a constellation. A portrait of George Washington hung from a chain on her neck; a "civic" band circled her waist. In her right hand she held a spear from which hung a band of wampum embroidered with emblems of peace and war. In her left hand was a scroll representing the Constitution. The carving was lost when the *United States* was dismantled in 1865, or perhaps in 1812 when the navy replaced figureheads with billetheads. It may be lying unrecognized and unclaimed in some loft or barn.

It is surprising how few tools were used to carve these intricate works of art: a gouge for hollows, rounds, and sweeping curves; large and small chisels for cleaning up flat surfaces; and the so-called "V-tool" for emphasizing lines and veining. A mallet and a special screw for fixing the work to the bench completed the list. William Rush used the tongue-and-groove method to fasten the parts together, and then, to add to the holding process, a five-inch spike of brass

87. Hercules, famed for his strength and power, is an example of a classical figurehead. *He* would be a protective spirit for a vessel. The Hercules figurehead as William Rush designed it for the frigate *Pennsylvania* is preserved in this drawing. Although the artist's concept included the entire figure, only the head was actually used. Heroes as figureheads stood on wooden platforms wreathed with acanthus leaves. The classical touch strongly influenced American carving. *Pauline A. Pinckney, American Figureheads and Their Carvers (W. W. Norton & Co., Inc., 1940)*

88. Male figureheads have always been popular, more so in Europe than in America. Even in this country, however, a sizable proportion of the figureheads were of men. This one is at the South Street Seaport Museum.

89. Another male figurehead—that of the *Silas Conby,* a Baltimore clipper used for cargo and passengers during the gold rush days. Later, after a collision in the Irish Sea, she ran aground and became a hulk. *South Street Seaport Museum*

90. The figurehead from the tea clipper *Algerine* gives the sense of dignity and respect carvers had in representing the male figure on a ship, especially in Europe. *South Street Seaport Museum*

91. Usually when a child appears as a figurehead, it is thought to be a son or daughter of the ship's captain. Child figureheads are rare, and always particularly appealing. *American Collector*

or wood. Some carvers used slanting grooves at the points where the arms joined the body, so that they could be removed in time of storm.

Native woods used were walnut, chestnut, pine. The fruitwoods—apple, pear, and plum—were especially sought after. In museums, you will find some carved from mahogany. When I asked Richard Orcutt, a carver who grew up in the shipyards of Maine, about the woods preferred for figureheads, he said: "Whatever good piece happened to be around. I've seen a carver, after looking a long time for a good piece, settle for a piece of pine. Carving was considered important, but even in my boyhood it didn't have the status it does now."

As in studying any work of art, one looks at details—the sweep of line, the unity of execution.

Many a figurehead on a whaling ship was carved by the sailors themselves, who joined to provide the vessel with a worthy prow or to replace a well-loved symbol lost in a storm. Generally, however, a figurehead was an expensive addition to a ship. Early American shipowners therefore kept records of such commissioned work. Thus, only in the United States are the names of large numbers of the carvers known.

Possibly nothing illustrates the interest in ship carving better than the furor and political strife that arose over the commission to Laban S. Beecher to carve a figurehead of President Andrew Jackson for the frigate *Constitution*, when she was undergoing a refit in 1834. Feelings ran so high that Beecher worked under armed guard, first in the Boston Navy Yard, and then, as fears arose for the figurehead's safety, in the New York Navy Yard, where he also worked under guard. But the carving was finished. Those who liked Jackson felt it was magnificent—the tall spare figure, erect and proud, with iron will written on the face. It was carved in what is said to be his riding costume, with a cape-cloak, a tall stovepipe hat in one hand, a roll of papers in the other (see Ill. 95). When the figurehead was completed, it was proudly mounted on the *Constitution*, which for safety was berthed between two other warships, with armed guards on all three ships.

Jackson's political enemies were furious at this success, but they were to be appeased. On the night of a heavy thunderstorm, Samuel V. Dewey, an anti-Jackson merchant skipper, rowed to the *Constitution* and sawed off the head of the figurehead. It was a daring political achievement. Rewards were offered for the return of the head, but it was too good a political prize. Six months later, after it had been shown in many a political meeting, cartooned and commented upon in many a newspaper, Captain Dewey, his mission accomplished, walked into the Boston Navy Yard and returned the controversial head. The body and the head were reunited, and the carving of Andrew Jackson sailed on the *Constitution* as its figurehead. However, it did not seem fitting to the secretary of state that a repaired figurehead should represent the President, so he ordered a new figurehead of Jackson to be carved. Although the representa-

92. American vessels with women for figureheads attracted a great deal of attention in foreign ports. To the astonishment of the world, American vessels were feminine. Some of these figureheads paid tribute to the best in American womanhood in the nineteenth century. There is a kind of feminine sweetness in this figurehead of the *Clarissa Ann* at the Bath Marine Museum.

93. Figureheads are still available—if you are willing to pay the price. This one with a touch of pathos about her pose began her career on a vessel in the early nineteenth century. She was bought in a New York antiques shop by the director of the Columbia River Maritime Museum, where she stands today.

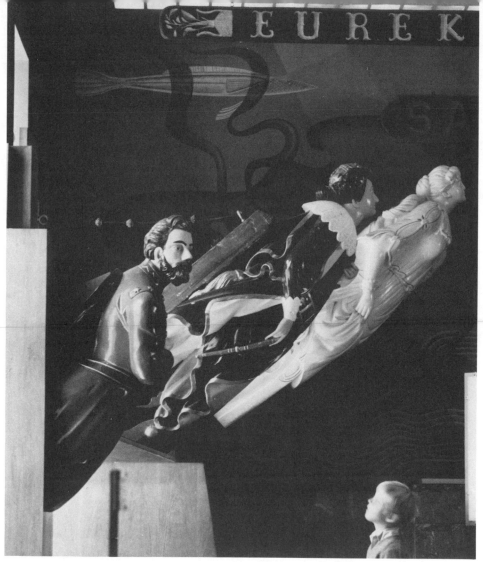

94. Something of the majesty, superstition, and veneration in which figureheads were held is hinted at in this display. *Photograph by Karl Kortum, courtesy of San Francisco Maritime Museum*

tion stood on the prow of the *Constitution* for many a year, it never attained the fame of the one that had been beheaded.

A truly popular figurehead (see Ill. 46) was that of David Crockett as portrayed by Jacob Anderson, an outstanding carver of New York City. The sturdy pioneer is shown in a deerskin suit, his rifle firmly clasped, his long hair flying free under his cap. His was a revered figure in the clipper ship era as the packet-clipper *David Crockett,* built by the Greenman Brothers at their yard in Adam Point, sailed the seas. She was among those fast-sailing packet-clippers that brought a new concept of speed to the slower-moving craft of Europe. Speed was the goddess of Americans, and her countrymen gloried in her "fast" trips to Liverpool, for she was a living, flying image of their inner desires. Later, this inbuilt speed, combined with successful winds and skilled masters, enabled her to make twenty-five trips around the Horn, some of which broke records. Today, as already mentioned, the figurehead of David Crockett has a permanent place in the collection of the San Francisco Maritime Museum.

Though figureheads of pioneers and Indians always attracted excited attention when ships bearing them docked in the ports of Europe, figureheads of women were the most popular of all in the sailing days of the nineteenth century (see Ills. 92, 93, and 96). In the monotonous nights at sea, sailors found it comforting to have a woman on the bow. But men as well as women were portrayed in numbers as figureheads of ships. Famous personages and some not so famous make up a long list: captains, owners, loved ones. As late as 1934 Joseph Conrad was carved as a figurehead for a vessel.

Various animals, mythological and actual, snakes, and birds also served as figureheads, but in the nineteenth century in America the truly esteemed one was that of the American eagle. A letter to the well-remembered Quaker shipbuilder Joshua Humphrey by William Rush echoed the country's feelings. He wrote that, of all the emblems for figureheads, he preferred the American eagle "darting upon and destroying the vitals of tyranny."

Particularly known as a fine carver of eagles was John Bellamy (see Ill. 98), who had his shop in Kittery, Maine, just opposite Portsmouth Harbor. (Late in 1973, a carved eagle attributed to him brought $2,750 at an auction of folk-art pieces.) In their day, Bellamy's eagles were found everywhere on ships: as figureheads, on stern boards, on gangway boards. A familiar roost was

95. This figurehead of Andrew Jackson was "beheaded" by Jackson's political opponents. The head circulated among patriotic societies for six months before it was returned to the Boston shipyard, where it rejoined the body to sail again on the *Constitution*. But the secretary of the navy thought it improper for a mended figure of the President to serve as a figurehead. A new figurehead of the President took its place—untouched by hot political feelings, and certainly more debonair. *Drawing by Louisette Barrett*

96. There is an especially appealing quality about this figurehead at the South Street Seaport Museum. Her name remains unknown, her ship lost, but like the many other figureheads, she deserves a salute across the barriers of time.

97. Eagles were probably more often used somewhere on a vessel than any other motif, so proud were Americans of their national emblem. They are found as life-sized carvings as figureheads on the bow, on stern boards, and over pilothouses. The Mariners Museum at Newport News, Virginia, proudly displays this fine example.

on the pilothouses of early steamboats. Their use was so extensive that they were often spoken of as "pilothouse eagles."

Unlikely to find such an eagle today? It can happen. My daughter and I came upon one in a small secondhand furniture store in Greenwich, Connecticut —and at a price we could afford! This eagle could not have been a figurehead on a vessel, for it showed none of the signs of wear of the sea. We call it a "pilothouse eagle." To the sailors in the early steamships, these pilothouse decorations had the feeling of figureheads on sailing ships. Our eagle has a wingspread of nearly four feet. It is carved of old dark brown mahogany, each feather distinct, its beak open, its wings outstretched as if it were about to take off. We do not know who made it or what ship it graced, but it shows the hand of a great carver.

Many collectors have discovered figureheads, but with the opening of more and more marine museums they are becoming scarcer on the market. Ours was a true find. We bought it at an unbelievable price—two hundred dollars for a masterpiece. Those that most dealers advertise cost much more, but keep in mind that you are buying *sculpture*. A well-known New York dealer offered one for sale in his catalog in 1964 for around a thousand dollars. In 1970, I saw one advertised by a midwestern dealer in nautical antiques for two thousand dollars. Considering their significance historically, and their scarcity, either one would have been a good investment.

Booth Tarkington found a figurehead in a garden, and bought it for his studio in Kennebunkport, Maine, where it stood until his death. It represents a young girl with flowing dress, the skirt picked up in one hand as she steps forward, her right hand on her breast just below where the curls fall over her shoulder. Her head is thrown back, her mouth partially open. Tarkington used to quip that she was "a young woman spitting to windward."

If you go looking for a figurehead, you may not find one. It is the way of

98. How ships flew over the waves, kicking up spume, feeling the cut of the wind as it filled the sails! Today it is possible to feel that rising sea and cutting wind again. At Mystic Seaport the *Charles W. Morgan* has been so completely restored she lives again. The *Joseph Conrad* beside her, though moored there in quietness, continues to fulfill its original purpose of a training ship as it serves as living quarters for youngsters who learn sailing in small boats. Mystic, a town and shipyard and a heaven for those who yearn to know nautical antiques, beckons with outstanding examples of the finest from the past. Here is a carved wooden eagle with staff and pennant, by the famous carver John Haley Bellamy (1836–1914). *Mystic Seaport photograph, Mystic, Connecticut*

99. The San Francisco Maritime Museum owns this impressive eagle figurehead. Eagle figure-heads were very popular. They were used so often on steamboat pilothouses that the term "pilothouse eagle" is almost a cliché.

so many antiques. By being elusive, they become more desirable. The figurehead from the Norwegian ship *Merkur*, which was wrecked on the Gaspé Peninsula in 1908, lay undiscovered in a house in Springfield, Massachusetts, for half a century.

Another subject of a dramatic rescue and contemporary fame was the eagle figurehead carved by Henry J. Purrington of Mattapoisett, Massachusetts, for the *Wanderer*. In 1924, when the ship sailed out of New Bedford, she had led the way for forty-six years. With the eagle at her prow, she seemed well nigh indestructible. When she was wrecked off Cuttyhunk, the men fought the high and treacherous seas and succeeded in saving their eagle. Brought back to New Bedford, the figurehead lived on in modern minds as a harbinger of good in the motion picture, *Down to the Sea in Ships*.

We have shown that these treasures of a romantic past are not unobtain-able. The problems for a collector are the usual problems of any collector of antiques: identification and authentication. Dating a figurehead by its size is dangerous. Figureheads were made and in popular use from before the Revolu-tion to the twentieth century. Figureheads that are five feet tall are classed as "small." The average for a full-length figure was seven and one-half feet. Ex-tant are some higher than eleven feet. Life-size figureheads date from Colonial times, but they continued to be used after steel sailing vessels replaced wooden ones.

100. An eagle that has all the earmarks of being the work of a great carver was found in a secondhand store.

Remember that even good reproductions can be expensive. They are made not to deceive, but to please. If antiquity and the sea are your passions, however, you could not do better for the central sculpture in your living room or study.

There are other ways of owning figureheads than to possess one physically. They can become a possession of beauty, a memento of days spent in some marine museum, of sorting and arranging their different charms, until you can say—that one is mine. My delight is a woman figurehead known as the Pine Lady, displayed in the New Brunswick Museum in Saint John, New Brunswick, Canada.

101. The proud quality of the American eagle stands out in this one from a pilothouse.
Brainstorm Farm Antiques

Figureheads lean out from the walls of marine museums in proud stance. American figureheads stand on a little vaulted platform, but English figureheads often come off the stem of the vessel itself. There is a typical stance for American figureheads: almost always one foot is ahead of the other. Sometimes it is only a dainty forward step; sometimes it is a dramatic step, as with the figurehead of David Crockett. One hand usually hangs free at the side. It may clasp papers, as does the figurehead of Andrew Jackson; it may hold a rose, or, like the famous Indian figurehead Seminole, a tomahawk. The other hand usually rests upon the breast.

This stance of a figurehead helps in dating one. The earlier ones tend to be upright. When they were carved for clipper ships they had a rakish way of bending somewhat forward; actually, they were carved to follow the line of the bow. Other figureheads appear to tilt their heads backward rather than hold them upright. This is especially true of the tall neoclassical goddesses.

The early figureheads were usually full-length figures; then three-quarter-length carvings became the rule, and, in the latter part of the nineteenth century, busts of famous men and women were very popular. There are just enough exceptions to these rules to keep any one of them from being a hard-and-fast means of identification.

102. This eagle from the flagstaff of a Great Lakes pilot boat was offered for sale at an antiques show. *Nina Hellman Antiques*

103. The cry of triumph can almost be heard from the open beak of this eagle, at the San Francisco Maritime Museum. Many of his kind have survived the sea and years of neglect only because eagles were so popular that they were portrayed in vast variety by countless carvers, often with fine craftsmanship.

In studying figureheads in museums, you will notice how carefully the carver used his wood so that the figurehead would withstand the waves. Some figureheads were carved out of a single piece of wood, but more often figureheads were carved from large blocks of wood, and the whole doweled together. It was a quite general practice to make the arms removable, so that the figurehead could be protected from the waves in a stormy sea.

In the earlier, more rounded vessels figureheads stood practically erect. As vessels became narrower, the figurehead leaned forward. By 1850, the time of the clippers, they were practically horizontal. The change in form came because a figurehead must always appear to be leading the ship, flying forward with its eyes fixed on the distance.

A massive feeling prevails in all figureheads, though it may be lightened by delicate carving of lace, braid, feathers. One notices, too, the effects of its seagoing days. Not only are there cracks in most figureheads, but the sharp lines are rounded and sometimes small parts are broken. Often, however, these have been repaired before this sculpture of a bygone day is put on exhibition. Repainting is almost always necessary. Careful research is done on the paint that was originally used; small amounts usually remain in spite of the salt and the wind. The effort is to give to each, gods and goddesses, women and men, lions and dolphins, some of the splendor of launching day, a reward for leading their vessel through "many a dreary and misty night."

Small wonder figureheads are the delight of collectors: historic enough for any scholar, artistic enough for many tastes, inspiring enough to make collectors bow with seafarers to their charm.

BILLETHEADS

To the American in the day of wooden ships, the words *billethead* and *fiddlehead* were as familiar as spark plug and battery are to us. Perhaps this is not an accurate comparison—or does it imply that we have few purely decorative adjuncts to our modern vehicles? Pleasure in form and beauty was a strong factor in the intricate carvings that went into the making of long-ago ships. Certainly the curvaceous lady or the stern captain, plunging ahead into the unknown and uncharted seas, had nothing to do with the actual mobility of the ship. They were pure visions of delight and emblems of pride to the master and crew.

Like figureheads, billetheads and fiddleheads ride the waves at the bow of the ship. They are scroll-carved blocks usually designed with three basic patterns—acanthus leaves, rosettes, and C-curves (the latter, literally, scrolls carved in the form of the letter C). The difference between a billethead and a fiddlehead is in the direction the curves take: the billethead curves turn downward or to the side; the fiddlehead curves turn upward.

105. This beautifully carved platform supports the figurehead of David Crockett at the San Francisco Maritime Museum. When the scrolls in a billethead turn upward, it is referred to as a fiddlehead. In any form, billetheads are desirable collectors' items.

104. As the tradition of centuries—the lavish use of carving on ships—lessened, billetheads were used more and more on the prow in place of figureheads. Today they are much sought by collectors for use as decoration. Their varied arrangements of scrolls, rosettes, acanthus leaves, and the well-tested C-curve make them desirable examples of the fine carving done here in the eighteenth and nineteenth centuries. This photo shows a mid-nineteenth-century billethead that was used in place of a figurehead. It is from an unidentified vessel. *Mystic Seaport photograph, Mystic, Connecticut*

Because they cost so much less than a figurehead, the United States Navy—in one of its occasional moments of economy—did away with figureheads in favor of billetheads. This was during the War of 1812. In 1907, when a final policy banning ornamentation was adopted, there were few sailing vessels (and consequently not many billetheads) on the navy list. There had been, however, increasingly lavish bow ornamentation on steam-powered men-of-war since the post–Civil War period. The dreadnaughts of the Great White Fleet bore gilded scrollwork and painted shields at the bow. The 1907 policy did away with this remnant of a more prideful and personal period in nautical affairs.

Collectors find billetheads very desirable, but they are hard to come by. They have been reproduced in modern times, for many a carver feels competent to carve a volute, a scroll, and acanthus leaves. Don't be deceived. Look for the signs of age and the softening effect of the action of the sea. Actually, good billetheads, because they did not seem so important, are often harder to find than other ship carving.

STERN CARVINGS

Fortunately for the determined collector of nautical antiques, the passion for decorating ships in the seventeenth and eighteenth centuries did not stop at prows but extended to the sterns, where low flat areas offered fruitful ground for the work. Although not so elaborate as those on French and English vessels, the stern carvings on American ships are nevertheless eminently collectible.

Eight windows on the lower deck and four on the upper deck could be surrounded with intricate carvings, and often were. The entire grouping then was surmounted by three carved lantern posts, with lanterns. In the heyday of ship carving, the stern of a ship looked like a small chalet.

With the nineteenth century, the carvings grew simpler. They were in low relief. Often the stern board was made of scrolls with a small eagle in the center. The characteristic pose for a stern board eagle was with wings widespread, its head turned, its beak opened to attack. An eagle of this design and mien, and the shield of a flag with thirteen stars and stripes, formed the decoration designed for the *Constitution*.

A gentler symbol also was popular—a woman's face, often that of the captain's wife, was carved in the center of the stern board. It was framed in acanthus leaves and embellished with scrolls reaching out to both sides of the ship.

These lavish carvings were hardly helpful to the sailors. Not only did they interfere with the movement of the ship; rigging often caught in them. Still, elaborate eagle carvings were popular into the 1850s. Not until after the Civil War did they become simpler. Today, they can be found only in racing yachts.

It cannot be said with certainty that a collector is more likely to come upon a stern carving than a figurehead, but the mythical law of averages points that way.

106. Drawings submitted by Rush for the stern of the frigate *Pennsylvania. Pauline A. Pinckney, American Figureheads & Their Carvers (W. W. Norton & Co., Inc., 1940)*

107. Stern boards can still be found by collectors. This one, discovered in a Rhode Island antiques shop, is now at The Mariners Museum in Newport News, Virginia. Some of the finest of early American portrait carving appeared on early stern boards.

108. Quite often the stern board was carved by the same craftsman who carved the figurehead. The high quality of stern board portraits provides evidence of the skill of these carvers, as in this example in The Mariners Museum in Newport News, Virginia.

109. An eagle with the insignia of the United States. Both were often carved for various ship decorations, but most commonly were used as stern carvings. *The Herald Corbins*

NAMEBOARDS

Collectors tend to lump together the carved pieces that identified old vessels as "nameboards," and so they are. Old seamen, however, referred to them according to where they were placed on the vessel. Trail boards, as the name indicates, trail aft from the figurehead or billethead on either side of the bow. The nameboards appear above them, close to the figurehead. Quarter boards are alongside the ship's quarters. A stern board goes all the way across the stern, sometimes being cut in the center by the rudder post. For example, the *Marie Celeste* would have a stern board with the name *Marie* on one side of the rudder post, *Celeste* on the other. Often there were other stern carvings.

Trail boards came first in use. They were scroll-carved in relief, with the name of the ship usually painted in gold leaf above them. Since the artist engaged to carve the figurehead also carved the trail board, the skill of the master's hand is generally reflected.

In 1812, the Congress passed a law that the vessel's name should be displayed on both the bow of the ship and the stern. This requirement resulted in the making of beautiful boards that have been a joy to collectors wherever they are found. They range up to twenty-four feet in length.

The Columbia River Maritime Museum at Astoria, Oregon, has a collection

110. These well-preserved specimens of nameboards—as the carvings carrying the ship's identification are generally known to collectors—are in The Mariners Museum, Newport News, Virginia.

111. Nameboards from a variety of vessels showing the beauty of the carved designs. Note the Stars and Stripes insignia on that of the *Louise Miles*. These hang on the walls of The Mariners Museum, Newport News, Virginia.

of more than two hundred (see Ill. 112). Curator Michael Naab tells of the time the museum staff was scrubbing up a donation of fifty or so nameboards outside the museum. It was hard to proceed with the task, as passing drivers stopped, fascinated at first, then covetous, wanting to buy.

Nameboard letters are well carved, sometimes in relief, sometimes incised and filled with gold, in order to be visible at a distance. Generally, two nameboards were used, but if there was only one, it was placed on the starboard side. In the absence of a figurehead, decoration at the bow of a vessel might be provided by a fancy nameboard.

Nameboards are still to be found by those who know their ship carvings. This was proved rather dramatically to my daughter and son-in-law, who have more than a casual interest in stories and relics of the days of the sea. As members of a seagoing family, with a grandfather who had been a master on schooners, and two granduncles lost at sea, they are constant visitors to maritime museums and special exhibits of nautical antiques. On one such trip to a museum they were looking at a display of trail boards when, to their astonishment, they came upon one with a familiar face looking out—a carved likeness of Grandfather Haley looking for all the world like his picture in the family album. The museum curator told them that the trail board had been found in a

112. The Columbia River Maritime Museum has nearly two hundred nameboards, ninety from a single collection.

113. A potpourri of nautical antiques from a recent antiques show. The eagle about to take flight is typical of carvings used on pilothouses and on the walls of the grand saloon. The trail board eagle, which seems ready to attack the figurehead, is from the *H.B. Smith.* *Kenneth E. Snow Antiques*

small antiques shop less than a hundred miles from their home. And at a bargain price.

Not so picturesque to our eyes as the square-rigger, the steamboat nevertheless was the pride of the nineteenth century, and it too had its share of carvings. In the beginning, many of the new ships carried figureheads quite as proudly as did the sailing ships. In time, because the bows were formed differently, the place of honor was shifted to the pilot house. And what more fitting than an eagle to crown it?

John Bellamy of Maine, as already mentioned, was a famous carver of eagles. Simplicity of line, combined with the intricacy of the feathered body and the gallant sweep of wings, gave the eagle figurehead supremacy in its day. Patriotism was high in the still-young nation, and the bald eagle and crossed flags appeared on ships from the Atlantic to the West Coast.

On side-wheelers, other areas served to display the carver's art. The box that enclosed the wheel bore carvings around its "breather holes." Inside, the cabins were ornate with carvings and gilt.

Catheads, which were used in hoisting the anchors to the rails, were also carved. A New Brunswick man told me of a curiosity he spotted in an antiques shop and left behind as merely that—a curiosity. It was a log from which the

Fig. 6. Paddle-wheel steamer. *Drawing by Louisette Barrett*

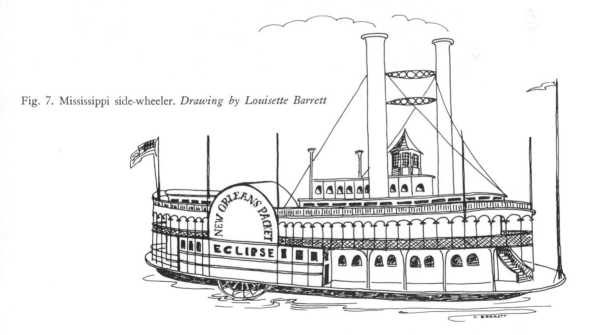

Fig. 7. Mississippi side-wheeler. *Drawing by Louisette Barrett*

bark had been removed, and had one end carved with a lion. Some time later it dawned on him that his forsaken find had been a broken cathead. A long-distance call to the dealer brought disappointment. The piece had been sold to a more knowledgeable antiques lover. So it is that the antiques we decide not to buy shine on in memory as masterpieces.

Even the gangway was carved, sometimes with eagles. We can see an example from the U.S.S. *Hartford.* With an open fan as the background, the dates of the ship's launching and its rebuilding are incised.

Among the most charming of the smaller carved ship parts are those on tillers. Though they are not plentiful, some have persisted into the twentieth century.

One marvels at the wealth of beautiful decoration. Perhaps it is because a ship is always "she"—never "it" or "he"—that so much loving care went into adornment.

A

114 A & B. Fish, the denizens of the deep, were another favorite symbol of early carvers. Some appeared on churches as a symbol of Christianity from early Roman days; some were carved with bold strokes for weather vanes. Others, minutely carved, served as wall plaques. They are treasured in almost any form by today's collector for the very vigor of their carving. *(A) The Herald Corbins; (B) Brainstorm Farm Antiques*

B

5

SCRIMSHAW AND OTHER SAILOR HANDCRAFTS

FROM MASTER TO THE LOWLIEST deckhand, no group of men worked harder under unbelievable hardships than sailors. In wooden ships with tall masts they set out from the ports of New Bedford, Mystic, Bath, Salem, Philadelphia, New York. The toll can be called up and down the eastern seaboard and, some years later, the western. They fought with waves a hundred feet high, faced death with the nonchalance that brave men summon when they confront the inevitable.

A sailor-cousin, whom I met at nineteen and have never seen since, made me *feel* what the life of a sailor meant. Late into the night I listened to his tales. Three times he had been the only survivor of the ships in which he sailed. As he told of his experiences, there was neither fear nor bitterness. Never before had I understood the call of the sea, its mystery and romance. We get glimpses of it in the trifles we collect. Landlubbers though we may be, we recognize that these are not really trifles but symbols of man's endurance and artistry. We touch with pleasure and understanding the smooth surface of whalebone carved by an unknown hand, marvel at the intricacy of a picture frame made of complex knots, look at a whittled square-rigger securely anchored in a bottle.

These are the monuments to the courage and toughness of the men who sailed the seas to Barbados and Canton, to San Francisco and Liverpool, to the South Seas and the Arctic for whales, for cargo that made shipowners and masters rich. And in the long, long hours when there was "nothing to do" they created such skilled handicraft that museums and collectors, you and I, seek it

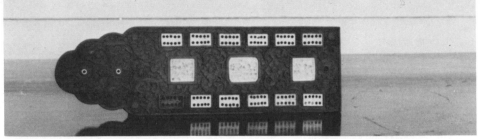

115. A seaman on a foreign coast, or walking through the woods on his day ashore, sometimes picked up a fine piece of wood. Then he created something like this—a cribbage board with inlay of whalebone. *Warren Long Collection*

out here and there and proudly display it today. It is the true folk art of the past, a folk art shared by all nations, yet particularly dear to sea-loving Americans.

Because scrimshaw, the art of carving and decorating small objects, is more typically American than any of the other arts of the sailor, it is justly famous. Scrimshaw, says Webster, is "to do any neat mechanical job," but specifically and nautically "to ornament, as shells, ivory, etc., by engraving." Somehow one does not think of the word as a verb, but that it is, though it also does double duty as standing for the "neat piece of mechanical work."

We think of sailors scrimshawing the hours away when not bending to the heavy tasks they had on voyages that sometimes kept them four years at sea. Many were illiterate, but the skill they developed out of boredom has been called by authorities the only wholly indigenous American craft. They scrimshawed any material that came to hand, including whales' teeth and walrus tusks (known as ivory), wood, shells, and the bones of many sea creatures. Because of the length of whaling trips, it was on these vessels, and with the parts of whales, that scrimshaw flourished.

After a whale was killed, the head and jaw were separated from the body with a razor-sharp tool called a spade. Drying and preparing the bones and teeth was tedious work, a process in which all participated in anticipation of the coveted carving pieces. The tools for scrimshaw were largely handmade; some-

116. Coconut was a strange new fruit to seamen. They whittled and carved in their spare time on any material at hand, even a coconut. The black shell of the coconut is finely embellished in this drinking cup. Occasionally you find coconut carving at a bargain price because it is unfamiliar to many collectors. *John Bihler & Henry Coger Antiques*

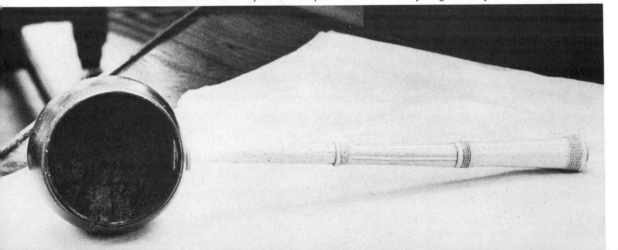

117. Here the entire coconut was used to carve a picture in relief. *John Bihler & Henry Coger Antiques*

118. Sailors brought home useful objects that would remind their sweethearts and wives of them while they were at sea. A rare find is this wooden rolling pin that was so carefully made and beautifully polished. *Warren Long Collection*

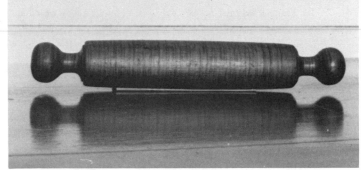

times only a sailor's knife was used. The whale tooth or bone was first engraved; then the design was picked out in India ink, soot, or lampblack.

It was creative work, and highly individual in form and quality. One hundred thirty-nine different kinds of scrimshaw pie crimpers have been counted (see Ills. 119 and 126). My grandmother had one made of whalebone that she used to crimp together the upper and lower crusts of her pies. As a child I was fascinated with it because of the bird carved on it. I wonder now what became of it. I hope it is in the loving hands of a collector of nautical antiques, and not lost through lack of appreciation and knowledge, a fate too often suffered by valuable old things.

Grandmother's other piece of scrimshaw might also have vanished into the unknown had I not been sentimental about this keepsake from her sewing basket —not often, I must confess, using it for its purpose. Again and again, it almost went into the box for the rummage sale or into the Salvation Army bag. From childhood I had spent my vacation with Grandmother. She was a great mender, and in my youth it seemed to me that she was always darning stockings using her light blue darner—called, in my memory, an "egg," for its oval shape. I vaguely remember her telling me that it had been made by *her* grandmother's husband. How I wish that I had asked more, but that statement had not impressed me.

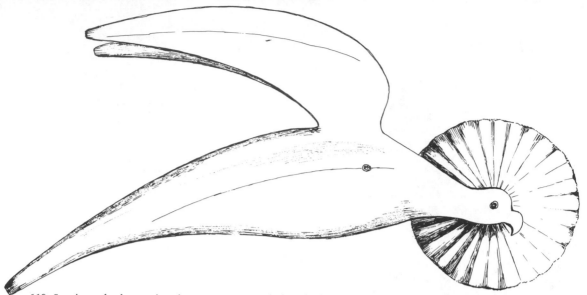

119. Jagging wheels, as pie crimpers were popularly called in the great days of whaling, were popular items for sailors to carve for their home folks. They are just as popular today with collectors. More than 139 different kinds of birds have been counted as jagging wheel decorations. This handsome bird made the cover of *The Magazine Antiques,* August, 1961, to announce one of their studies on nautical antiques. *Drawing by Louisette Barrett*

120. When every gentleman had a cane, one with a scrimshaw handle—or even an entire cane made of whalebone carefully worked into strange shapes—was an item of high fashion. These were delicately carved and skillfully designed, frequently displaying an imaginative spirit. Possibly because the handles were "attached," more has survived of this scrimshaw than of the work of seamen in other fields. *Kenneth E. Snow Antiques*

Grandmother's darner was deceptive. Most of the black that had outlined the carving had vanished in a century and more of use. Only if you looked with the greatest care could you see the lion's head (undoubtedly the ship's figurehead), a ship, a whaling scene, and part of the date 1811. Dated scrimshaw is rare (see *The Magazine Antiques*, September, 1972). So is scrimshaw that a sailor has colored blue!

To that gift from my Grandmother, with interest compounded, I owe in part my knowledge of nautical antiques. Scrimshaw is valuable, some quite *ordinary* pieces bringing up to one hundred dollars. (If Grandmother's darning egg had turned up in a rummage sale, I doubt that it would have been marked at more than a quarter.) Very fine pieces of scrimshaw may sell for as much as several thousand dollars today.

Opportunity waits for all collectors who prepare themselves by study.* Curiosity, reading, and field trips to museums are the route to great discoveries. But, as with all expensive antiques, there are pitfalls to be avoided in the search. Museum directors warn against outright frauds. With prices high and manufacture by machine now possible, scrimshaw may not be what it seems. The director of the San Francisco Maritime Museum says: "Many dealers are bringing in scrimshaw from England. True, it is sailors' work, but it is not our American craft."

One of the reasons that modern scrimshaw does not command the price of that made on the old sailing ships is that often mechanical means are used to speed up the engraving process, but there are modern workers who do the work by hand. Alan A. White is among these artists. His work is widely respected. He spent an entire winter completing one set of walrus tusks. Scrimshaw made in whaling days, however, has not only the value of the fine workmanship but the romance that inevitably accrues to such a piece.

---

* On September 11, 1974, the *New York Times* carried a feature article, "Wildlife Laws Are Hindering Collectors," which explained the effect the Endangered Species Act of 1973 was beginning to have not only on collectors but also on many antiques dealers, some of whom have ceased to market certain categories of objects. Among these are articles made of whale's teeth (scrimshaw), tortoiseshell, and various furs and leathers.

121. Like elephant ivory, the tusks of walrus and the teeth of whales have been sought after throughout history. Some excellent carving appears on pieces of walrus tusk. This one, signed "Tho. Worth," was so highly valued the eagle in the center section was outlined in gold. *Ellen Fales Lomasney*

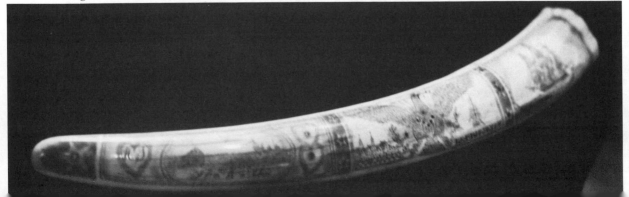

122. Whales' teeth are prized as some of the finest folk art of sailors. Meticulous workmanship was lavished on the carving. Almost always they are expensive, but to a collector a well-done piece is worth the price. This sperm-whale tooth was made to be presented to Lafayette Lodge (a Masonic lodge). *Harris Diamant, Eris Antiques, Inc.*

123. The ship *Audrre* out of Salem, Massachusetts, embarked on a whaling voyage in 1859 with Benjamin Webb as master. So strong were the home ties that, although the ship dominates the scene on this scrimshaw, a view of New Bedford is on the reverse side. This piece was priced at $4,000 at an antiques show. *John Bihler & Henry Coger Antiques*

124. A scrimshaw swift, most useful in its day, most effective in its conception—an outstanding treasure today. Small wonder collectors say "scrimshaw" in almost hushed tones. *Mystic Seaport photograph, Mystic, Connecticut*

In buying scrimshaw, especially if the price is high, the collector should
be very cautious. The modern scrimshaw that is engraved with power tools can
be deceptive. Study as many genuine pieces as possible. Practically all maritime
museums have collections, but there are few that compare with the display at
the Whaling Museum in New Bedford, Massachusetts, for many years a center
for the whaling industry. In the collection of the Nantucket Whaling Museum
there is a fine engraving on a whale's tooth of a sailor's conception of the victory
of the U.S.S. *Constitution* over the *Guerrière*.

Much cozier is the thought of a sailor sentimentally decorating a set of stay
busks for his lady back home. The stay busk was a corset stay, a narrow flat-
tened strip of whalebone, usually twelve to fourteen inches long, that passed
down the front of the corset. These were generally ornamented with scenes of
ships and whaling events, hearts and flowers, or simply geometric designs. Stay
busks, not surprisingly, with their warm and intimate association, were a popular
scrimshaw subject. But then so were utilitarian rolling pins, napkin rings, knit-
ting needles, bodkins, clothes pegs, birdcages, and walking sticks.

Many factors enter into the price of scrimshaw. I asked an experienced
collector for his opinion. "Each piece varies," he said, "for in each piece different
factors enter. It can cost $80, or $800, or $8,000."

Among the factors that add to the value of scrimshaw are its age, the proof

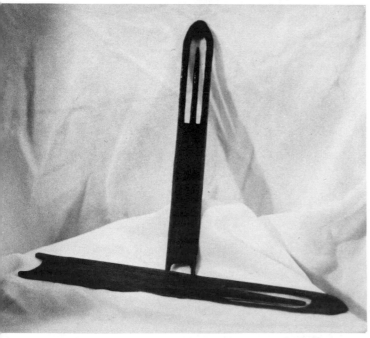

125. Net shuttles, used to work on and
mend nets. Even into small items
like these, seamen put much careful,
painstaking work. *Nina Hellman
Antiques*

126. An intricate example of scrimshaw;
the top of this pie crimper is removable. *John Bihler & Henry Coger
Antiques*

127. This scrimshaw puzzle has defied the efforts of everyone who has owned it and tried to take it apart. Perhaps only the sailor who made it knows the secret, and the secret is gone like the sailor. *Village Green Antiques*

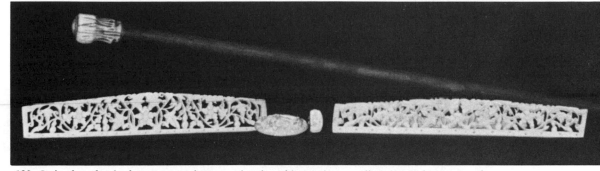

128. Scrimshaw knobs for canes can be expensive, but this one in a small antiques shop cost only a dollar. These pieces from ladies' bags, intricately carved, were brought up from a wreck of a whaler by divers off Hawaii.

that it was made on an American whaling ship, the fineness of its carving, and the interest of the subject.

I asked a man who for many years had sailed the Great Lakes whether the sailors on the lakes had done any kind of scrimshaw.

He shook his head. "You'll have to ask the men in the museum in Detroit," he said. "They'd know about it."

"But what did you do in your spare time?" I persisted.

"Oh, we used to whittle a lot," he said. "Some of the men would draw and paint, or carve things if they could get ahold of the right kind of wood. Sometimes we used wood from cigar boxes."

The sailor was not alone in his bewilderment about the term. The carving of small objects in a variety of materials is not generally known as scrimshaw. Generally the term "scrimshaw" is associated with carving parts of the whale not commercially valuable and thus expendable for sailors' handcraft, but it has been extended to include wood carving as well as the more difficult art of carving in ivory (walrus tusks and whale teeth) and bone. Be alert for objects and ornaments scrimshawed in wood.

BOXES

Among my own treasures is a box beautifully carved and inlaid with ivory that I took to be Oriental. Puzzled by the interior, which was typically Victorian jewel-box in feeling, I studied museum pieces and found that I was the possessor of a fine piece of wood scrimshaw.

These other activities of the sailor in his "spare time" should not be passed by lightly. They too are folk art. Although little attention has been paid to this kind of carving, in its care and delicacy it deserves a place in our collections. There are boxes in many kinds of wood other than the conventionally used cigar box. You will find them in maple, cherry, and birch, among others.

Not all these intriguing small boxes were the work of sailors. Many dealers along the Great Lakes call them "tramp work" because they were made by men who had no regular jobs (see Ill. 132). The word "tramp" was a familiar one in the late nineteenth and early twentieth centuries. Quite often it did refer to

129. Round ditty boxes took a certain skill to make. This example with the whale on the cover is exceptionally fine. Often ditty boxes were divided into sections in the interior. *John Bihler & Henry Coger Antiques*

130. This ditty box with an incised star illustrates another type of decoration sailors used. Such boxes are highly sought, but often can be picked up in antiques shops for small sums. *Orcutt Collection*

131. This large oval ditty box made of pan bone (from the jaw of a whale) had a wooden bottom. Although the lid is missing and the piece is in considerably less than perfect condition, five ships and the date 1776 are engraved on it—an extremely interesting and rare piece. *Nina Hellman Antiques*

132. Bureau box with an added jewel case on top, made by a sailor on the Great Lakes about 1850 from cigar-box wood, just as sailors on the oceans made ditty boxes from rare wood from the Orient. In the antiques trade such carving as this is known as "tramp work." When steam took over from sail, many sailors became tramps. Perhaps the name "tramp work" verifies boxes of this type as the ditty boxes of the Great Lakes.

133. Another such box, made of beautiful maple, has come down as an heirloom from the Great Lakes.

134. Most ditty boxes made on the Great Lakes were of fair size. The large one here is unusual in its workmanship and is fitted inside as an elaborate sewing box. The small round box is of the kind so often classified with scrimshaw, for the type was made on the long whaling voyages. Carved and hollowed from a single piece of wood, it is called a "sweetheart box." A similar box at a recent auction brought a price in four figures.

men who had been sailors, many of whom were put out of work when steamships took the place of sailing vessels. Up and down the Atlantic coast, mechanical ways were installed for doing the work that had once been done by sailors' hands, and the men who had been sailors became a problem. (It is hard to recall what we called such jobless people in those days; perhaps we referred to them as "charity cases" or "public charges.") Formerly they had been able to ship out to sea on almost any vessel. Now, there was no place for them. "Tramp work" may well come to be regarded as the scrimshaw of the Lakes; in any case, it has begun to rise in price today.

Many other boxes, of course, can be classified simply as "ditty boxes." These were the small ones sailors made to accommodate their personal possessions. Every sailor had such a box—they are as varied as the men who made them —designed to hold cherished possessions and practical items such as needles, thread, soap. Usually they are partitioned. Some were round, and some were square; some were carved and some were plain. Some were of very fine wood, others of scrap wood picked up here and there.

The strange woods that could be found in Far Eastern ports were often carefully worked into gifts for loved ones. The wood was always well polished; sometimes it was inlaid with other strange woods, or with ivory or whalebone.

A box that I greatly admire is made of maple. The interior is divided into three compartments, but its beauty lies in the way the maker used the wood, patterned, as one occasionally finds hard maple, with a delicate seaweed spray enclosed in the natural curl of the wood, known to us as curly maple.

That quite ordinary material—straw—was also most effectively used by sailors in decorating boxes. On one box, said to have been made about 1800, a harbor scene of colored straw decorates the lid. Inside there are scenes of the sea, also made of straw.

FANCYWORK

Fancywork, the art of doing embroidery, custom has related to women, rarely to men. Yet in the days of the sailing ships men too found pleasure in embroidery. Their skill in mending sails carried over into the making of beautiful embroideries.

In the restored *Balclutha,* docked close to the San Francisco Maritime Museum, which sponsored and restored the ship, can be seen embroideries, shawls, crocheted and knitted articles, all the work of sailors. To the observer they seemed like work done by women. I asked one attendant how one could tell they were sailors' work.

"We have their history," he replied. "All were made while the men were at sea, just like other sailors' handcrafts that are so treasured today."

But how many embroidered pieces will one find that have such a history, I thought. It seemed to limit the field for collectors. To my surprise, at the next large antiques show I attended, I noticed several offerings of sailors' embroideries.

"How do you know this is the work of a sailor?" I asked a dealer.

"Oftentimes you can tell a sailor's work by the materials," was the reply. "If you study a piece carefully, you'll find something in it that will show it's a sailor's work—usually the materials and the way they are handled. The piece may be delicate, but it's strong in feeling."

A second dealer explained: "A great many embroideries made by sailors are framed. To the sailor, such a piece represented hours of work. Sometimes he made a frame of knotted rope, sometimes of carved wood or a fancy piece of wood he came upon."

"The subject matter is the giveaway," another dealer said. "You can scarcely

135. A yarn picture of a ship made by a sailor is considered a prize by collectors. *The Stradlings*

136. One recognizes yarn work done by sailors by both the fine workmanship and the subject matter. This embroidery of an eagle and the flag is a superior example. *Orcutt Collection*

rank them as sailors' work unless they have a nautical background. Women may embroider pictures of ships, but they look quite different from those made by men. Nine times out of ten, a man's embroidery will have an entirely different character. Look at the sails and the rigging—and the details. Men see differently from women. Flags and ships and eagles were all favorite motifs used by sailors."

"The embroidery itself is the best guide," declared a fourth dealer. "Age and the sea leave their marks. A nautical embroidery that hasn't been framed is likely to be pretty fragile."

Lest you think these sailors' embroideries are only interesting trifles, you should know that an embroidered portrait of a frigate with a small image of the ship in the distance, as in painted portraits of ships, sold at an auction recently for $275. The delighted buyer carried it home as the prize of the afternoon.

ROPEWORK

Ropework is likewise referred to as the fancywork of the sailor. In its best expression it is powerful and effective. For many years ropework was not fully appreciated, and many fine examples of this work of the sailor have been lost through lack of appreciation.

Sailors had a natural skill with ropes—splicing, mending, and braiding rope were part of their daily chores. When they turned to fancywork, all this built-in skill came to the fore. The rope handles they made for chests are sometimes works of art in themselves (see Ill. 139). Rope was also used to good effect to decorate boxes, to make picture frames, to decorate parts of the ship. A friend of mine found an oarlock muffled in ropework ten inches long, extremely decorative because of the skill and variety of the knotting.

Excellent examples are displayed in the marine museums. In the Bath museum in Maine in one corner of our country and in the San Francisco Maritime

Museum on the West Coast, some very interesting examples of sailors' knotwork can be seen (see Ill. 80). In both the Whaling Museum in Cold Spring Harbor, Long Island, and in the Columbia River Maritime Museum in Astoria, Oregon, are to be found outstanding examples of the seven hundred knots or more that sailors used, in special weaves and splices. If you examine similar exhibits carefully in marine museums in any part of the country, you will find that the starting point is the knot: cube-shaped, flat, raised, or round.

Knotwork called by its technical title of macramé has had widespread resurrection as a craft. Men, women, and children are making it today. The Museum of Modern Art in New York gave the revival impetus when, a few years ago, it displayed in its galleries modern work side by side with the great work of the men of the sea. With this seal of approval, many began tying knots. Craft stores today have supplies and books of directions for becoming an artist with knots.

By watching the children in a summer camp, I discovered that although the starting point is just a knot, tapestries, hangings, necklaces, and many other articles can be formed by a series of patterns endlessly involving the knot. These patterns that stretch backward in time, formed by sailors with rope, are indeed varied. With the young campers, two patterns were especially popular, one in which the strands were woven into a spiral and another known as the "Turk's head knot," a turban woven into a herringbone. Two patterns are a far cry from the seven hundred knots and splices some sailors were said to do, but all are beautiful whether combined in a hanging, a bracelet, or a muffled oarlock cover.

137. Sailors perfected knotwork. Some of the effects that could be achieved by tying knots are illustrated in this display from the Bath Marine Museum.

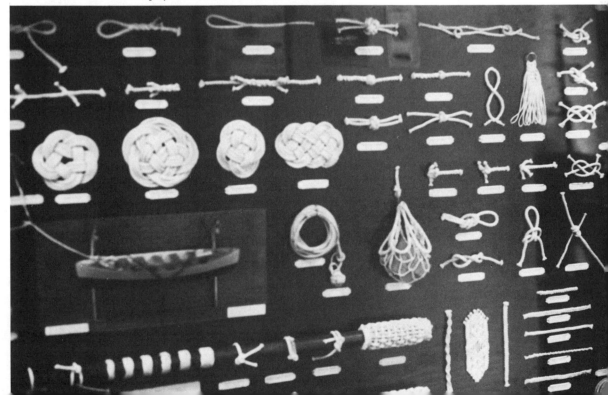

138. Knotwork and beckets. These examples, displayed at the San Francisco Maritime Museum, show the similarity between knotwork on the West and East coasts.

139. In the opinion of collectors, skillfully woven beckets (the sailors' name for handles) "make" the sea chest. *Orcutt Collection*

140. This rope for the gangplank was used when the master walked on board. *John Bihler & Henry Coger Antiques*

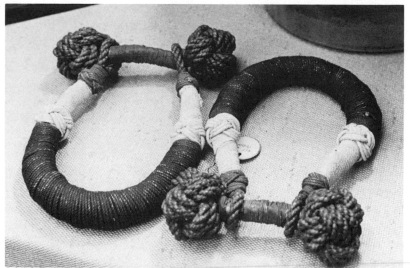

141. Macramé is beautiful whether made in the 1850s or the 1950s. Here are red, white, and blue beckets, carefully made. *The Herald Corbins*

142. Knotwork over rope holding parrel beads is seen here in the San Francisco Maritime Museum. The parrel secures the boom as it swings from side to side on the mast.

143. A superior example of nautical handles of a different sort that have been converted into bookends. *Ronald Bourgeault Antiques*

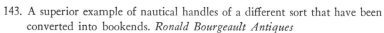

Because of the ephemeral nature of paper, few examples of paperwork are found. Yet paperwork was among the arts practiced aboard ship in the cramped quarters a sailor called his own. There were two kinds of this work: paper cut out in intricate forms and mounted on a colored background of paper, and rolled paperwork. In the second type, small tightly rolled pieces of paper formed the material of which a sailor composed his picture.

Some years ago, in a marine museum, I saw a full fleet of ships cut in silhouette and mounted against a sheet of blue paper. Its beauty still haunts me, though I have never been able to recall just where I saw it. A placard at the side said it was work done in the late seventeenth century.

Certainly, as the early sailors made these many and varied pieces from paperwork to scrimshaw, they did not realize they were creating works that would be sought and treasured by museums and collectors a century and more later. Few of these men could read, yet their industry and skill left for us a great heritage, perhaps more lasting than most of the so-called "great things" the shipowners hoped to accomplish.

144. Rope and knots decoratively frame a shadow box half-model of the schooner *Beate* in the Columbia River Maritime Museum.

6

OTHER IMPORTANT
COLLECTIBLES

PARTS OF SHIPS

THE SHIP AND ALL ITS parts have tremendous pull on the imagination of collectors. Museums, aware of this, have actual vessels anchored at special piers, and bring into their displays all the varied components of the ship. For example, just inside the entrance of the Cold Spring Harbor Whaling Museum in Long Island is a fully equipped whaleboat that visitors can board.

The San Francisco Maritime State Historic Park displays, among others, the *Balclutha*, a typical British merchant ship of the late Victorian period. Inside the museum there, an exhibition of parts of ships can be examined—the fife rail, the pumps, and a section of the mizzenmast from the four-masted schooner *Forester*, for example. The *Forester* is of special interest in the area, having been built at Alameda and long served on the Pacific coast.

These ships and parts of ships in museums have had a decided effect on the collecting public. Many feel that actual contact with ships of the past is causing the groundswell of interest in collecting nautical antiques. Private citizens—increasingly—are bringing parts of ships into their homes. So it is that, though collecting figureheads, stern boards, and other ship carving is not new, the trend toward ship's pumps, hatch covers, and skylights is still novel.

For ideas on things to collect, you can do no better than visit maritime museums and study their displays. On exhibit you may well find billetheads, wheels, spars, anchors, nautical ironwork, cabin tables and benches, skylights, moldings and fittings, and even major examples of cabin joinery. This may sound like a formidable list, but it indicates many interesting possibilities. A house-

109

wrecking company in Stamford, Connecticut, finds it more profitable to sell parts of ships than parts of houses. The company bought all the hatch covers from several Liberty Ships of World War II, and sold them for tabletops. You could buy one as a finished table, a refinished tabletop, or an unfinished one.

Speculators have bought up parts of the *Queen Mary* and the *Normandie*. Some parts they stored. Others were converted into bookcases, end tables, cabinets, even small items like bookends—a strange fate for the two mighty liners

145. Sails that once blew with the sound of a cannon shot are tattered and gone today. Rotted pieces may come to light, or a folded sail tucked in a trunk years ago and preserved there since. The lines that whistled in the wind sometimes remain, and rope ladders, rope beckets, and the ropework of sailors. *Photo of Annie C. Ross by P. L. Sperr, courtesy of The Mariners Museum, Newport News, Virginia*

that carried so many thousands between America and Europe. Yet their glory lives on. In the case of the *Queen Mary* and the *Normandie,* these tangible symbols give the feeling of the past, an aura of authenticity, more effectively than pictures or words.

Many an ingenious collector prefers to find his own mementoes, and convert them to use. Friends of mine, swimming in the Pacific, found that what seemed to be a piece of driftwood caught in the rocks was a partly submerged rudder made of wood and copper. They dove and pulled to get it free. Its size and workmanship led them to believe it was from a yacht. However, their research failed to bring a single clue—the sea keeps its secrets well. Though the vessel remains nameless and unknown, the rudder, enhanced with a few pieces of mahogany, graces the living room of one of its finders as a coffee table.

Wheels, so naturally decorative in form, are eminently collectible. Most desirable are the ones that are brassbound, with brass hubs, bespeaking the careful workmanship of a good ship or yacht. Sometimes a wheel is rough when found; the sea has done its work. The surfaces should be refinished as carefully as in a fine piece of furniture. The best method of preservation is to apply several coats of a mixture of equal parts of boiled linseed oil and turpentine, with an interval of forty-eight hours between each application.

A dramatic use of a ship's wheel is exemplified by the great wheel of the *Brother Jonathan* (Ill. 146), which greets you at the entrance to the Dan and Louis Oyster Bar in Portland, Oregon. The story goes that when the wheel was brought up by divers years after the ship was wrecked off Crescent City, California, on July 30, 1865, a dead man's hand was found clinging to it. The wheel may be the only part of the *Brother Jonathan* to have been recovered. Louis Wachsmuth, who with his brother and their sons runs the restaurant founded by the original Louis C. Wachsmuth in 1919, thinks so, but is not sure. For an authentic account of the wreck of the *Brother Jonathan,* he recommends Lewis and Dryden's *Marine History of the Pacific Northwest,* edited by E. B. Wright, Portland, 1895. A rare copy of this old history reposes in a specially made case high on the wall of the Oyster Bar. Only the proprietor has the key.

The feeling of reverence for a ship's wheel and an old volume of nautical history are the keys to the difference in this quiet seafood house. It is a small museum in itself. The interior was planned years ago to represent an actual ship's interior. Walls are knotty pine. Lights are old ship lanterns, most of them wired, but some in their original state. Starboard and portside lights shine to right and left at an entrance. There are three large ship's bells, which give forth distinctly varying sounds when pulled. An engine-room clock "bought from an old sailor forty-five years ago" is on one wall. Three port lights from the battleship *Oregon* are set into walls. Louis Wachsmuth deplores the dismantling of the *Oregon* to provide scrap iron in the anxious period of World War II, but adds that the dismantling was a windfall for collectors. Parts went for seventeen cents a

146. Sometimes a story goes with a ship's wheel. One of the worst disasters along the California coast took the lives of all on board the *Brother Jonathan*. Only the ship's wheel remains today to tell the tale. It stands at the entrance of the Dan and Louis Oyster Bar in Portland, a restaurant decorated exclusively with nautical antiques.

147. The steering wheel from the lighthouse tender *Manzanita*, which was stationed for many years at Tongue Point. Almost every marine museum displays a wheel that once responded to the helmsman's hand in foul weather and fair. *Columbia River Maritime Museum*

A

148 A & B. A seaman reached for a belaying pin as an object of common use, but today one is a collector's prize. These are on board the *Lizzie G. Howard,* docked at South Street Seaport. Many a museum displays a deadeye; here (*B*) we see a deadeye attached to its chain plate at South Street Seaport Museum.

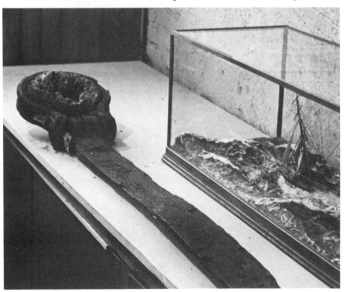

B

149. Note the hand-turned rail on the *Maude Palmer,* in dry dock in this illustration. Occasionally these rails come to light today with all the beauty of the wood and the carving preserved. *Photograph courtesy of The Mariners Museum, Newport News, Virginia*

pound. Hundreds of plates, prints of shipping subjects galore, cases with shells, models, and miniatures line the walls of the Oyster Bar; they are the only decoration. The plain deal tables are ungraced by cloths or vases of flowers.

Anchors are always sought, but many are so heavy that getting them to the place where you want them to be is sometimes a problem indeed. My friend, Mrs. A. J. Hathaway of Wilson, New York, on Lake Ontario, found this out when she purchased a house built in 1840 by Captain Johnson, a well-known Great Lakes master. One of the captain's ships had been wrecked in Lake Ontario. Years later, when the state was dredging near the lakeshore, one of the wrecked ship's anchors was brought up. In homage to the captain and the heroic shipping days of the past, the anchor was taken to the home he had built, and installed on the front lawn.

When Mrs. Hathaway bought the house, she thought well of the prize that went with it, an anchor in the yard, but decided she would rather have it as an ornament in the gardens. She had not reckoned with anchors. In spite of modern equipment, it would not be budged. So the captain's anchor still stands high in the front lawn, ready to tell the world its story—and many there are who ask and listen.

Other strange things found in collections include rails, skylights, and companionways—these last often made in their own homes by joiners, the aristocrats of carpenters. Many parts of ships mirror the loving craftsmanship of the men who made them. They not only made vessels of utility but equipped them with separate parts of great beauty.

Tall masts took exceptional skill. America's stands of virgin timber provided the material for work that went all over the world. Reminders remain in our cities for those who have eyes to see. They are the old flagstaffs, of which the greater number were fashioned by the mast makers. The same dexterity with axe and drawknife, the same eye for a tapering line, were needed for both.

I take great pleasure in the flagstaff in the center of Mystic's business area, and still clearly recall the day that I stood watching as the colors were lowered. The slanting rays of the sun, the breeze from Mystic River, and the tall, tall mast were for me poetry, romance, and tall ships. Look reverently at the next flagstaff you pass—you will feel those things too.

150. When you go on board an old ship, sometimes you find that the finish on the wood is extremely well preserved. Here is a skylight on the *Wavertree* at South Street Seaport Museum.

151. An unusual part from a ship is this piece of the mizzenmast and boom from the schooner *Forester* at the San Francisco Maritime Museum. You can see how the boom rotates, upheld by the collar secured to the mast. The fife rail and pumps are also preserved in this display.

152. Wheels, rudders, booms, masts—large and ungainly, but made of wood— have been preserved by salt water through the years, and all are displayed with pride at maritime museums. The section of a square-rigger's yard shown here, with the massive iron truss that secured it to a mast, is at the San Francisco Maritime Museum.

153. Heavy, hand-wrought chains that once held an anchor are used for decoration outside the Sword & Shield Restaurant at Lake Chautauqua, New York. This is a treacherous little lake, subject to violent storms; many a chain curls in the mud at its bottom.

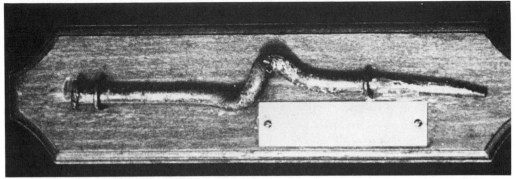

154. It takes special connections to acquire such an unusual nautical antique as this mounted copper spike that hangs in the small sitting area off the kitchen in the home of Mrs. William C. Wilson, Portland, Oregon. It was a gift to her husband, the late Lt. Comdr. Wilson, Ret., and bears the following inscription:

COPPER SPIKE REMOVED
FROM WOODEN HULL OF THE
USS HARTFORD

LAUNCHED JAN. 22, 1858
DECOMMISSIONED AUG. 20, 1926
DISMANTLED NORFOLK, VA. 1961

155. A bare boom silhouetted against the sky shows a block still in use on board the *Lizzie G. Howard* at South Street Seaport Museum. Other blocks that once did the work for seamen lie on shelves in museum stores and antiques shops across the country.

NAUTICAL INSTRUMENTS

As many other antiques for use in the home are the province of women collectors, so things connected with navigation's past are the delight of many men
collectors. In dens and family rooms as well as offices, the artifacts of the sea
are appropriate—some used for purely ornamental purposes, others as bases for
lamps or parts of useful furnishings. Perhaps more important than the decorative appeal of old instruments is their tie with the past. One touches hands with
those who worked to discover ways to make navigation safer—an impetus to
collecting found in few other specialized fields. The sextant you find may have
played its part in a journey to the Far East for spice, to the New World for
liberty. But the precision and beauty of these old instruments also are part of
their appeal. It is hard to believe that they did the job so well. You sense their
quality when you stand on the replica of a ship's bridge in the Museum of Science
that overlooks the Charles in Boston and see how far navigational instrumenta-
tion has come, as you study the latest marine navigation equipment aboard—
radar, course recorder, gyro pilot, loran, sonic depth recorder, rudder angle indicator, bearing repeater, master gyro compass, and radio direction finder. Still,
how far and well they sailed the seas before the dawning of the scientific era!
Small wonder old navigation instruments are cherished, and that their cost is
going up and up. Not long ago a good reproduction of an octant, made in England, sold for $150.

In many museums, the importance of early navigational instruments is
dramatized in displays. Some are fortunate enough to have paintings of a ship's
captain with his instruments. The Penobscot Marine Museum in Maine exhibits
a painting of Captain Benjamin F. Mecher, a model of his clipper ship, and the
maps, parallel rule, and compass by which he charted his course. In the Bath
Marine Museum, Maine, you will find an oil painting of a ship built by Houghton
Brothers of Bath correlated with the compass and parallel rule used by her skipper, Charles E. Reed of Richmond.

These examples in early paintings and engravings are important because
no instruments exist from medieval times and few from the fifteenth, sixteenth,
and seventeenth centuries. But, alas, the sources for these are almost as hard to
come upon as the instruments themselves. You should know their value, though,
for occasionally one does find old books, as well as pamphlets, in which nautical
instruments may be represented on the cover page or even appear in the text,
with delightful line engravings. The earnestness of man's effort is mirrored in
this news item from the *Royal Gazette* of December 5, 1781:

> M. Evans compliments to those men whom he has taught Navigation and
> requests the favour of their company from 6 to 7 o'clock in the evenings
> during the winter having a few hints to give them in that art, particularly
> finding the latitude by the altitudes of the sun and the Longitude by the

distance of the moon from the sun as exhibited in John Hamilton Moore's NAVIGATION.

Early books on navigation are an intrinsic part of any collection. Outstanding among them is the *New American Practical Navigator*, written by Nathaniel Bowditch at the beginning of the nineteenth century. The book made two significant contributions to the science of navigation: it laid down for the first time a simplified method of working out positions, and it provided correct and

156. The nautical telescope or "spyglass" has been called the instrument of discovery. It consists of one tube or a series of tubes. A particularly appealing representation of the early telescope is the mariner's weather vane shown here, which was found in the upper Hudson Valley. Made of rolled copper, this outstanding piece of American sculpture glorifies an instrument that played an important part in building the country. *John Bihler & Henry Coger Antiques*

usable tables of previously unheard-of accuracy. Bowditch presented navigation as a practical skill that could be learned by any reasonably intelligent seaman.

The *New American Practical Navigator* rapidly became known as "the seaman's bible." Revised, updated versions are still in use by modern mariners. All early copies of the work are collectors' items, and expensive. Even somewhat later editions are sought—and snapped up quickly—by collectors.

Many books played important roles in early navigation. A knowledgeable mariner today would not feel comfortable with an almanac as his one navigational tool, but Brown's *General Almanac* brought many a farmer from New Brunswick to the lime pits of Maine. In their homemade boats, popularly called "Johnny woodboats," they carried tons on tons of wood to be used in making lime, from Canada to Maine, with nothing but the almanac as a guide. What charm even a dilapidated copy of Brown's *General Almanac* would add to any collection of nautical antiques!

The search for nautical instruments to make navigation safer first bore fruit in the Mediterranean in the middle of the twelfth century and somewhat earlier farther east. About that time it was found that a magnetized needle floating in a bowl of water always pointed north. Then, for the first time, men could determine their course over the trackless waves without depending solely on winds and stars and sun. These needles gave way to hard-steel needles that held their magnetic attraction, and the water compass soon evolved.

Because the compass has meant so much from that day to this, it has long been the delight of all nautical collectors. An interesting adjunct to the compass is the binnacle—a case, box, or stand containing the compass and a lamp for use at night. The earliest binnacles were shaped like a conventional chest or cabinet, having a chamber for the compass and another for an illuminant. By the late eleventh century they had evolved to their present form—a hooded chamber for the compass, atop a pedestal. The bases are often made of fine hardwoods; the cover surrounding the compass is usually of brass or copper.

Quite early in the history of the compass its card or dial became standardized. There was usually an eight-pointed star as a part of the dial. A relatively new addition is the calibrated outer dial, and the fleur-de-lys that ever marked the north. The dials of early compasses were brightly colored—beautifully engraved, with the calibrated segments often painted red, blue, green, or yellow. This gay dress began to disappear about the middle of the nineteenth century, when some compass dials became black and white.

In the long roster of the many different types of nautical instruments, some successful, some unsuccessful, the chip log and line ranks as the most enduring. It was a practical device for estimating a ship's speed through the water, and so effective that it was in use from the twelfth century until the last days of the sailing ship. With a vessel steady on its course, the line calibrated with knots was heaved over the stern. The number of knots run out in a minute by the sandglass showed how fast the ship was moving. Chip logs and lines have passed with the ships that used them.

Plate 1. Antonio Jacobsen, the famous American painter of steamships, had his own particular style. *Lake View Galleries*

Plate 2. Shown here, along with a picture of the Burgess homestead in Somerset, Massachusetts, are mementos of the *David Crockett,* owned by Captain Burgess, who was also part owner of the clipper *Challenge.* His prized octant is still in the family. *Persis Pettis Hall Collection*

Plate 3. Square-riggers are the models most loved by collectors and model builders. *Orcutt Collection*

Plate 4. Knowledge of the stars is an absolute necessity to navigation on the open sea. Celestial globes like the one shown here aid the novice as he learns the stars.

Plate 5. Shadow boxes with a ship model and a background and foreground are set off by the box and frame. They are judged by the perfection of their detail. *Orcutt Collection*

HUDSON RIVER DAY LINE.
BETWEEN NEW YORK AND ALBANY

Plate 6. A chromolithograph of a vessel of the Hudson River Day Line, a byword in the East for fifty years. *Orcutt Collection*

Plate 7. Mah-Jongg set made in China. The lacquered case contains carved ivory tiles. *Gordys Vidler*

Plate 8. This pilothouse eagle sailed on a tug before it settled down over the front door. *Orcutt Collection*

Plate 9. An old ship lantern can be made into a hanging lamp for a home. *Orcutt Collection*

Plate 10. Some nautical antiques find their place outdoors, like this schooner that seems to sail again high on the barn wall. *Orcutt Collection*

Plate 11. One of the finest of Michele Felice Corné's works; he painted it on wallpaper in a home in Newport, Rhode Island. *Newport Historical Society*

157. Nautical compass at the Columbia River Maritime Museum. Compasses are old instruments that changed very slowly; thus most nineteenth-century compasses closely resemble this modern example.

Another relic of the days of sail is the traverse board, on which helmsmen recorded the speed and course steered during a watch. These boards were not large. An eighteenth-century example has on it the traditional dial of the compass with its calibrations, and on the right-hand side a pegboard marked in half hours for pegging the vessel's speed.

So many types of navigational instruments were made in the long search for greater safety that all of them can scarcely even be enumerated. One man who had sailed many ships from the South Seas to the English Channel declared: "Most of us who love the sea are delighted with any old nautical instrument we come upon. Part of the fun is figuring out how they worked, and what their purpose was."

Most of the early instruments are very decorative, and extremely rare. When the long-sought Spanish galleon *Nuestra Enora de Atocha* was located off the coast of Florida in July, 1972, the Smithsonian Institution was willing to forego the gold that was plundered in the New World—the pieces of eight and other treasures spilled on the ocean floor when the galley sank in 1622—if they could have the astrolabe. An astrolabe was designed to make it possible for the mariner to discover his position at midday by determining in degrees the height of the sun. This circular instrument, with a stem, crossbar, and a movable indicator that pointed to the degrees engraved on the rim, was designed so that it hung plumb no matter how much the deck of the small sailing ship might heave. Some astrolabes were of beautifully chased and molded brass.

It is estimated that less than a score of astrolabes are in existence today, so the collector is not likely to find one; but if you come upon any round, well-decorated old instrument, hang onto it. Even if it is not an astrolabe, you can be sure you have a prize.

There are many instruments, such as the sandglass and surveyor's instruments, that today we scarcely think of as having a nautical past, but they were

158. A sandglass, before the days of clocks, was essential on land and on sea. On board ship it was important as a means of measuring the rate of speed. *Nina Hellman Antiques*

important to mariners during the seventeenth, eighteenth, and nineteenth centuries (see Ills. 158 and 159). French surveying instruments of the seventeenth century are very valuable—they were so well made and of such elegant design. English-made instruments from the eighteenth century are preferred but any navigational device is a collector's delight.

These early surveying instruments enabled the navigator to make more accurate charts. This was graphically illustrated in the map made by Dutch navigators in the late seventeenth century, which for the first time showed lower California as a peninsula instead of an island.

As various types of navigational instruments were being developed, the great search was for an accurate timepiece to tell time at sea. One such device was offered in an advertisement that appeared in the *New York Gazette and General Advertiser* of July 23, 1799:

NAUTICAL INSTRUMENT PERPETUAL LOG OR DISTANT CLOCK

The proprietors by a patent granted under the Seal of the United States of America for the discovery of a nautical instrument called a Perpetual Log or Distant Clock to find a ship's way at sea take the liberty to inform the Public that they have appointed Bulmain and Dennies, No. 59 Water Street, their sole agents for vending of the above described instrument, in this State. By them alone subscriptions for the same will be taken, and information given respecting the terms. N.B. One of the above mentioned instruments may be seen at the Bar of the Tontaine Coffee House.

Seeking to fill the need for a sea clock, the Royal Society of Great Britain offered a prize of twenty thousand pounds to anyone who could develop an accurate and reliable chronometer. The prize was earned by John Harrison, an Englishman, in 1765. Earlier, Thomas Godfrey, in America, and Dr. Edmund Hadley, vice-president of the Royal Society, in Great Britain, had, in 1731, simultaneously developed the principles of the quadrant, which became known as the "Hadley Quadrant." Quadrants, octants, and sextants are used for measuring angles—between celestial bodies, between the earth and celestial bodies, and so on. The sextant became so important to navigation that every ship's master

159. An early protractor, used to plot a course or a position on a chart. *Nina Hellman Antiques*

160. Most sextants include a small telescope. This sextant was owned by Captain George Julius Nielsen in the early 1900s. Torpedoed on the U.S.S. *Covington* in World War I, he managed to save his sextant, which is now owned by his grandson, Roger G. Williams.

161. A close-up of the most important instrument on board ship: the sextant. Note that the telescope at the right is part of it. *Rhode Island Historical Society*

162. Late-eighteenth-century ebony and brass octant in a step case, with the name E. M. Hazard on both ivory inset and case. The inside cover has a painted brig; on the outside, an eagle in dull gold bears a banner in his mouth with the name of Evan Hazard. Above the eagle a Masonic emblem suggests that Hazard belonged to this fraternal order. *Mystic Seaport photograph, Mystic, Connecticut. Photograph by Lester D. Olin*

163. A sextant that illustrates what to look for: a well-worn case, a label, an instrument that shows signs of having been used. This one is of particular interest because of the New Bedford label, although it probably came from England originally, where most of the best sailing instruments were made. *Nina Hellman Antiques*

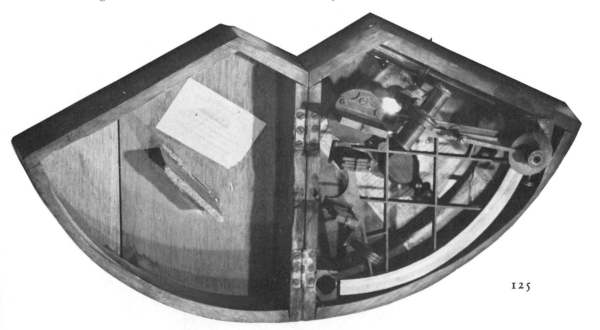

was required to own one. Since sextants were very expensive, the cost sometimes prevented a qualified man from becoming a captain.

If you plan to collect nautical instruments, investigate some of the many technical books that describe them. The maker's name always increases the value of an old instrument. American makers' names are rare because in the early days most navigational instruments were imported. Oftentimes a line of descent can be traced from a maker's name. On a kidney-shaped box was the name of John Berge. The collector was fascinated, did a bit of research, and turned up these facts: Berge lived from 1742 to 1808. He resided at 55 St. Paul's Church Yard, London, England, and was apprenticed to Peter Dolan, then to Jess Ranson. Only collectors can appreciate the excitement such discoveries can bring.

It takes considerable money to collect the early nautical instruments and something of a purse to collect even the later ones. Many factors enter into the prices asked for old instruments. They need to be in working order, or in such shape that they can be put in working order. One is worth more if it is in its original case, and if the original case is decorated or has something unusual about it, the price is higher.

The curator of a nautical museum remarked to me a bit sadly, as he looked at an auction sale catalog of nautical antiques, including nautical instruments, "I'm not planning to go, for with such high quality the prices will be too high for me. We'll have to wait till the buyers of some of the present-day rarities decide to give them to our museum."

Yet, even though your purse is lean, you may still own some very fine

164. Another type of a ship's compass. A label adds greatly to the value of an instrument. This one reads Kelvin & Wilford O. White Company, which had offices in Boston, New York, and Montreal. *Nina Hellman Antiques*

165. A barometer that came down in the Haley family. It was rescued by Captain Frank Haley when his ship went down in the most adverse circumstances, yet his wisdom saved the crew—and the barometer.

166. The ship's binnacle, used to house the compass. This one is at the South Street Seaport Museum.

167. Anchors are a more common antique, but impressive. They often meant the saving of a ship in storm or in trouble, which adds to their significance today. This one was photographed on board the *Lizzie G. Howard* at South Street Seaport.

things. With nautical antiques as with others, a collector discovers that the knowledge of what is good quality, significant workmanship, and good materials can mean more than money. This happened to my daughter, who was a student of astronomy. On a table of junk in a thrift shop was a celestial globe on which the constellations had been engraved. The paper was hand-colored and gored to fit the globe. There was a well-calibrated and beautiful horizon ring, also well-turned brass legs that reminded one of the turnings on old candlesticks.

These globes were used in the seventeenth and eighteenth centuries to teach sailors the constellations they needed to be able to identify at sea. As nautical science evolved, the globes were not taken to sea so constantly, but they were long used as a nautical aid for teaching on land.

The moral is: Learn what you can about old navigational instruments and don't be dismayed at the prices that are often asked. Just keep searching. Even today, when interest in them is high, you are sure to find some that you can afford and will greatly enjoy.

◄ 168. The dial of a ship's telegraph, by which the captain sent orders to the engine room, is now a decoration of the Dan and Louis Oyster Bar in Portland, Oregon.

169. A different version of a ship's telegraph, now on display at the Columbia River Maritime Museum. Note the small handle at the left; it was used in guiding the ship by indicating directions to the engine room.

NAUTICAL FURNITURE

The term "nautical furniture" is a loose one. It applies to the furniture of the ships of the seas; but, as all boat owners know, nautical furniture can be just land furniture transferred from home to the decks, to be hallowed by the sea. It becomes antique nautical furniture when it has taken on the salt air, traversed the sea, and then escaped the destruction of going down with the ship or being brought home and "forgotten."

Oftentimes the furniture can be quite splendid, judging by written accounts of the *Congress,* one of the early frigates. William Rush had eloquently urged that the figurehead be Wisdom, "Congress being the great legislative body on which the majesty of the Republic alone can rest." Prominent citizens came across with gifts. Benjamin Burke, the silversmith, furnished pieces of plate and silver spoons. The poop lanterns were the gift of Levi Haws, a well-known ship chandler. The decanters were the gift of James Tucker. And so the list went, but everything was "elegant." It was that way with the other frigates.

If one looks at the French Empire dolphin sofa, part of the original furniture aboard the U.S.S. *Constitution,* and now roped off in the Smithsonian Institution, one surmises that for important vessels, furniture in the height of fashion was chosen. The taste in furniture was still the same two decades later, as illustrated by the furniture from the luxury yacht *Cleopatra's Barge,* now in the Peabody: by 1820 the sofa had become lyre-backed with more carving

170. During a gale, passengers and furniture were tossed together in the grand saloon of the *Great Eastern.* Every movable piece of furniture was broken, including all the chandeliers. This three-day gale in 1861 made headlines when the battered vessel limped into port. *Harper's Weekly* gave it the best of coverage. Prints showing the interiors of ships are rare.

171. The interior of a schooner inspired this drawing. In coastal vessels not everything need be anchored, but casualties to furniture seemed to be as great, judging by how little has survived. *Drawing by Margery Reeves Kinley*

and was a bit heavier, but it was still French Empire.

Eighty years later, however, taste had indeed changed. By the 1900s, we see in the captain's quarters of the restored *Balclutha* comfortable late-Victorian furniture. There are "throws," as they were popularly called, draped over some of the pieces. There are also outstanding examples of sailors' "fancywork," well done and typical of Victorian elegance.

In large measure, ships were furnished—as far as the captain's quarters were concerned—by the captain's wife. And from the days of Queen Anne to those of Queen Victoria, wives chose, to the best of their ability and means, what was fashionable.

We scarcely think of our cane-seated chairs as inspired by the China Export Trade. (The cane used to weave chair backs and seats is split rattan.) But during the period when ships were making fortunes for their owners with cargoes from China, cane-seated chairs were very much the thing. Undoubtedly, caned articles were nautical furniture on some sailing ships.

Judging by the variety of desks that turn up in family collections, all kinds from all periods went to sea to become "the captain's desk." But the type generally referred to as a campaign desk (for the campaigns on which the British infantry and cavalry officers took them) has recessed brass handle pulls on a body divided into two parts, so that it could be carried on and off the

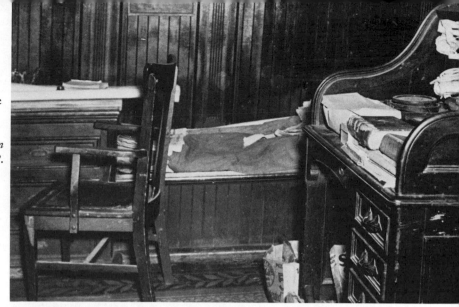

172. Furnishings in a cabin aboard a schooner may be sparse but they are serviceable. *Photographed on the Frederick P. Elkin by William T. Radcliffe, courtesy of The Mariners Museum, Newport News, Virginia*

ship easily. What is properly known as a captain's desk is a small, more conventional desk, usually with a slanted top, and drawers on one side of the kneehole.

The usual captain's chair is more standardized. It is a form of Windsor, with turned legs and a low back about twelve to sixteen inches high held up by spindles an inch or more thick. Around the top center of the back is another piece of wood—sometimes three—in the form of a collar; that is, they turn back on themselves and give a certain grace and finish to the chair. Occasionally, the thick plank seat is slightly shaped.

The earlier chairs may contain three different woods: basswood, maple, and pine; as the nineteenth century wore on, the chairs tended to be made entirely of maple. By the 1890s, they were being made by machine. Factory-made chairs in this style are referred to in the antiques trade as "firehouse chairs." They did furnish many a firehouse, but they also were used on riverboats and steamers.

Another type of ship's furniture was made especially to fit very specific dimensions and was built by some of the ablest joiners of the day. Since joiners were the best carpenters, they were always assigned the most exacting jobs. They built tables, chairs, desks, and beds, but few of these have survived. A furniture designer, seeing some that had escaped the dismantling operation, exclaimed, "Modern furniture at its best, and to think it was built a century ago!" It had to be well designed to make the best use of every available space in the ship.

Often used on shipboard were small lap desks. I had one that came down in the family. It must have been English, for it was beautifully inlaid with holly. It was said to have been done on shipboard, and the elaborate workmanship makes that seem most likely.

Classed with nautical furniture are many smaller items. The potbellied stove (see Ill. 177) and kitchenware from the galley are cherished today. The medicine chest has meaning for some. Mirrors are scarcely articles one thinks of as nautical furniture, yet a surprising number of seafaring mirrors have sur-

173. This "captain's chair" that once had its place on a vessel on Lake Erie varies considerably from the usual type. The handles on the top of the back were used for moving it. The chair was found in a barn. *Fenton D. Moore*

174. The water cask, so precious to seamen, is shown here below decks on board the *Lizzie G. Howard* at South Street Seaport Museum. These early casks make fine tables and good conversation pieces.

175. The fire barrel, much less precious, stood on deck ready for use. This one is at South Street Seaport Museum.

176. Besides the elegant nautical furniture, there is also the utilitarian. A cooking stove, now on board the *Wavertree* at South Street Seaport Museum, indicates why a good cook was so prized on board. He worked against obstacles—not just the sea and limited food supplies—but his stove as well.

177. On cold wet days it was always difficult to keep warm on board, even with the red glow in the pot-bellied stove around which the crew gathered whenever they could. South Street Seaport Museum displays this example.

vived. After all, if one could not see the home folk, it was probably pleasant to glimpse a familiar face.

Like other furniture in the captain's cabin, mirrors were in the favorite style of the time. One in the Bath museum and one that came down to my daughter from her husband's forebears are quite similar (Ill. 178). Both are in the style of the early 1800s, with pilasters on the sides that uphold a pediment. Beneath this is a reverse painting on glass. A narrow bar separates the painting from the mirror below. The mirror my daughter has was handed down for several generations. The original owner willed it to her son's wife with the comment: "She'll cherish it if she's worth her salt."

Although wall and shelf clocks can scarcely be classified as nautical furniture, speaking of the reverse paintings on glass used to decorate mirrors brings to mind the large number of such paintings used as door tablets on clocks. Quite a good many of these featured ships. An exhibition by the Concord (Massachusetts) Antiquarian Society included a handsome banjo clock made early in the nineteenth century by Lemuel Curtis, with a door tablet picturing the *Constitution* and the *Guerrière*. Other famous ships as well as unidentified ships likewise were painted in reverse on glass for clock tablets.

Of course the sea chests, which were made usually by the sailor himself, are the most familiar of all nautical furniture. They practically prove their own authenticity.

178. Mirrors reflected the style of the time. The so-called architectural type of mirror changed little in appearance and decoration from 1750 to 1800. This example with a nautical scene at Bath Marine Museum is typical of the period—a painted upper panel and the cornice with thirteen molded balls.

SEA CHESTS

The sea chest was a sailor's own particular nook on board ship. Not only did it hold his clothes and small belongings; it was a place for him to sit. Most chests are a standard size: eighteen inches deep by eighteen inches wide by three feet long. The lid overlaps. The hinges are stout; and two strong rope handles at the sides make for easy carrying.

These are the similarities. In decoration, the chests are as varied as their makers. Here we have true folk art. The museum examples fill a collector's soul with desire to own one for himself. In the antiques market, sea chests are far from cheap, and prices are going up. Probably nothing would surprise the original owners more than the prices paid for their handiwork.

Influencing the desirability of these chests are the stories their decorations tell. In many cases, a sailor's painting on the lid of his sea chest is the only known likeness of the ship on which he sailed. The favorite place for a painting was inside the lid, a spot protected from wear (Ill. 181). Usually these are waterline paintings of the ship riding on simulated waves or against a background of blue.

I saw an especially beautiful chest at an antiques show. It was made of teakwood and inlaid with whalebone. The use of teak indicated that this particular sailor had made the trip to the Orient and returned home safely. It had, in the field of antiques, that special credential that makes a piece desirable—and extra expensive.

179. This is the sea chest of Captain Samuel Crocker, handed down in his family. In a letter to his wife, he wrote: "It seems to me I never wanted to see you so bad as I do now. If I could be with you I should feel like a new man. . . . I wish you was here to get a good sail and I'd give you a good kiss as well." Because of his love for her, he had decided to quit the sea and this was to be his last trip down the coast. He left his sea chest home because part of his return journey would be by train. It was one voyage too many. His ship sank and he never came back to the woman he loved. *Paul and Mavis Crocker Collection*

180. At South Street Seaport Museum is the sea chest of an apprentice, Philip Dudley Carey, who sailed around the Horn in 1905 when he was only seventeen, on board the *Loch Garry*.

I have a beautiful chest in which the Pennsylvania Dutch influence is strong. Painted tulips arise in special compartments from the base, three along the front, two on each side, and three on the top. It is well made, with good dovetailing, rope handles, and overlapping lid, and it is the size of a conventional sea chest, but it is certainly also a dowry chest. On it are painted the initials of the bride and her bridegroom, and the date 1778. Did the sailor paint it for his love while he was at sea? Or was it made in the likeness of a good sea chest, after the marriage, to hold the bride's precious linens?

181. The appeal of sea chests stems partly from their artistic decorations in the folk-art style of the period. The painting of a sea scene on or under the lid of such a chest is often a real prize. On this example, the decoration on the front, including the initials and a man and a woman, suggests it may have been built as a hope chest for the seaman's beloved. Many sailors built chests for this purpose. This one is also interesting because it is dated (1837) and has good beckets. *Brainstorm Farm Antiques*

182. This painting in oil on sailcloth, once on the top of a carpenter's box, is of the lumber ship *Dirigo,* famous because Jack London sailed in her and wrote the major sequences for *The Sea Wolf* as a result of the experience. *Gary C. Cole*

Other chests were used at sea too. The ship's carpenter had a chest for his tools. An interesting chest has a picture on the sailcloth used on its cover; this was a carpenter's chest on the ship used by Jack London as the basis for his story *The Sea Wolf* (Ill. 182). I was told of an eighteenth-century seaman's chest, picked up in Spain for a moderate sum, which was covered with votive-offering pictures. It seemed unique to me, but I have since heard that, in Spain, one does find such chests.

An advertisement in *Down East* offered a sea chest with a painting of a ship inside the lid for two hundred dollars. At a good, but not elite, Fifth Avenue auction, a chest was bid up to more than five hundred dollars. In a small antique shop, one was priced at ninety-five dollars.

They are hard to find, but if you want one it will turn up sooner or later. That's the way with antiques.

LANTERNS AND LIGHTS

Cherished by all lovers and collectors of old things are the candles, lanterns, and lamps that shed light in the days when there were no switches and circuits to bring immediate clarity to the scene. The contrasts between now and then are especially dramatic as we think of sailors and ships on dark and boundless seas, and study their lamps and lanterns in museum displays. No wonder collec-

183. One cannot always be certain whether a lantern was used on board ship, since so many different types were used over the years. This one is unusual because it is signed by its maker—I. Reed. The date 1854 is on it also, with one number on each side of the top. *Ellen Fales Lomasney* ➤

◀

184. Candlesticks, hand carved by a seaman. *Barbara Vollmecke*

tors seek and treasure the lighting devices of other days. For light on a ship, sailors often had to depend on only a piece of blubber in a fire pan, just as early colonists had to resort to the light of burning pine splints in their homes. Fire pans are often listed in seventeenth-century Massachusetts inventories.

Candles were the chief source of light, in both candlesticks and lanterns, until they were displaced by the kerosene lamp after the Civil War. In Gloucester fishing boats, they were mounted in iron sockets with two spikes, one vertical and one horizontal. Lamps had quaint names—the Betty lamp was sometimes called the "slut" lamp; the Cape Cod spout lamp was a descendant of the Flemish spout lamp.

The most picturesque lights were the three great lanterns carried on the sterns of sixteenth- and seventeenth-century naval vessels. Crowning the beautiful carving of the period, they are a delight to see even in pictures. They faded away with the discontinuance of elaborate carving.

The early ships of the Colonies carried poop lanterns on the poop deck, the aft part of the ship. You will find them in models of the period, or in prints. Lanterns—or lanthorns, as they were originally called—are choice collectors' items. They were an integral part of the ship—its protection, its means of com-

185. A whale-oil lamp designed for use on a ship as either a table or a hanging lamp. *John B. Kierner III*

186. This whale-oil lamp was taken from the *South America*, bought by the United States government in 1861. It authenticates that whale-oil lamps of this type were used on vessels of all kinds. The reservoir and wick are made to swing freely, so that they will be in an upright position even in rolling seas. *Drawing by Diane Foster*

187. Double-wick pewter whale-oil lamp from an early ship. John Miles, in 1787, discovered the principle that made these lamps possible. They were immediately adopted in America. Like most great discoveries, this one was very simple. A reservoir for the whale oil was fitted with a burner consisting of one or more tubes with solid wicks. The lamp was economical and clean. Pewter was the most desired metal for high-class lamps, but lamps were also made of tin, iron, and brass. *The John A. Reardon Collection*

munication, its illumination. Similar in form, they vary greatly in detail. They are as old as candles, their original source of light. Those on Colonial ships were made of tin, or tinned sheet metals. In 1793, Thomas Passmore of Philadelphia advertised "lanthorns" among seventy-seven tin objects to be sold.

188. This signal light from the mid-1800s was used on the Connecticut River. It is now at South Street Seaport Museum.

190. One of a pair of running lights from a large sailing vessel. Running lights were used on the sides of a vessel— one on the starboard and one on the port side. *Orcutt Collection*

189. Lanterns were usually made of galvian, a very heavy tin that was painted black. The two smaller lanterns at right were running lights, a pair being needed on a vessel. The largest lantern is partly made of brass, which is unusual. It also has the maker's name on the bottom. The smallest lantern, at far left, is also a running light. *Orcutt Collection*

Early lanterns were simple affairs—a square, round, or oblong box with translucent horn for panes—and thence came the name *lanthorn*. As panes of glass become common in the eighteenth century, the name "lantern" came into frequent use. About this time, too, turreted tops and ornamental trim were added, and the plain tin lantern was reinforced at the edges with soldered wire. The tin was sometimes plain, sometimes perforated in patterns of stars or other designs. Often the lanterns were painted on the outside, leaving the shining tin surface inside to reflect the light.

The discovery of tin-plating sparked the use of iron for the body, to give added strength. The seventeenth-century process was to hammer a small ingot of iron into a sheet. This was done by a worker called "a beater." The sheet was cleaned, then dipped into a vat of molten tin. This plated tin was strong, attractive in its silvery color, and it did not rust.

I asked an old seaman about ship's lanterns. "Why," he said, "they were made of tin. Sometimes pierced." But of course we know there were also brass and copper lanterns and combinations of tin, brass, and copper, largely made for yachts and other luxury ships.

Lenses of blown glass, connecting a base and a top of tin, are typical of lanterns used on ships in the eighteenth century. In the nineteenth century, colored lenses were often used instead of clear glass. Port and starboard running lights are red and green, respectively. An ingenious collector who found a pair in an antique shop puts them to use every Christmas season, to the left and right of the entrance to her home.

191. The lighthouse without a light. So popular were lighthouses in the last century that this one was built at Niagara Falls, although no vessels sailed there. *Gleason's Pictorial Drawing-Room Companion, 1850*

Few of the earliest lanterns have a maker's name (see Ills. 183 and 189). Those that do are more valuable, but any ship lantern is desirable. It is a nautical antique that, in many a form, can "do things" for your home. Old ship lan-

192. When Minot's Ledge was washed off its foundations in the "Great Storm" of 1851, it was a catastrophe as great as the loss of a ship. This light, built to take its place, has stood ever since. The former light lies at sea, buried with other nautical antiques in the silent deep. *America Illustrated*

terns are also sought by boat owners, who prefer those that have come down through the years to new ones.

Marine museums are making some very fine reproductions, and they are frankly sold as reproductions. Buying them helps the museum, and good reproductions can develop your taste for the real thing as nothing else does.

193. The revolving lens from the North Head Lighthouse now reflects the indoor lights at the Columbia River Maritime Museum.

COMMEMORATIVE POTTERY AND PORCELAIN

By the time any pottery or porcelain is a hundred years old or more, it's commemorative of something. Consider, for instance, the charming straight-sided cups found in a wreck in the New Brunswick River. These few eighteenth-century dishes—all that remain—make one think of the disappointment of the housewife who was looking forward to having an entire set, and of the hardships and privations of making a home in this new wilderness world. And what of the

194. Liverpool pitcher, transfer ware, probably circa 1800, on one side bears the name *Sarah Mutter;* the other is decorated with a ship under sail. The pitcher is eight and one-half inches high and has a two-quart capacity. *Mystic Seaport photograph, Mystic, Connecticut*

captain and men of that long-forgotten ship? Did they make it to shore?

However, such is not the strict interpretation of the term "commemorative." True commemorative porcelain was made to celebrate special events. In the late eighteenth century and a good part of the nineteenth, people were interested in greetings and commemorations. "A good trip to India" is found engraved on one of Wedgwood's famous punch bowls. Another offers "Greetings to Captain Perry." If the family could afford the luxury, commemorative cups and saucers were also made for family events such as the birth of a baby. Of course there were many engravings and decorations on pottery and porcelain to commemorate naval victories. On a famous Liverpool pitcher there is a toast "To the crooked town of Boston."

All this whimsy delights collectors and makes them look at old pottery and porcelain with a new feeling. It will help you as a collector if you know the principal makers of commemorative ware, but it is when the artist has used a ship as decoration that collectors of nautical antiques are most excited by discoveries of seventeenth- or eighteenth-century pieces. More often than not, these masterpieces—and they well may be just that—are safely couched behind glass in museums. Still, old things do come down in collections, eventually to reach owners who do not appreciate their worth and hence put them up for sale. It happens in every field, but probably more often in pottery and porcelain than in others.

Artists have been depicting vessels on these fragile materials for centuries. In fact, the first painting we have of a boat is found on the inside of a cup painted in the sixth century B.C. by Exekias. Now in a German collection, it shows a little boat with a single mast and a bannerlike sail. Two oars are anchored on the high prow. There is even a figurehead; the stem curves around a birdlike figure. In the decorated stern, Dionysos, lying on cushions, enjoys the glories of his sacred grapes as he holds a wine cup in his hand.

What a joy it is to see—for example, on a plate—the ship *Friendship* of Salem painted just as she started out, with smoke coming out of her gunports, her sails catching the wind, and the American flag flying high and proud. The whole scene is encircled by a Chinese border. The plate is in the Peabody Museum collection. One small plate can recall a sweep of time, the clipper ships, and the export ware of China, as well as the fortunes that were made. Plates arrived, were used, and are gone in the poetical dust of the centuries.

Liverpool pottery, with its ships and comments, seems to be more available than China export ware. Perhaps my viewpoint is colored because I've owned a Liverpool pitcher decorated with a ship in full sail, but never a heraldic plate or cup that came from the land of Far Cathay. As the name implies, Liverpool pottery was made in England. The factory, established in the eighteenth century, flourished largely because of the American trade to which it catered. Ships were the most typical decoration of the ware. Tiles and other forms were made, but most familiar to collectors are the pitchers and punch bowls.

Black ship prints against a creamy, yellow-white body characterize Liverpool wares. In some places, blue or other colors may appear in a border, but generally black on creamy white is the distinguishing characteristic. If you've never seen this ware, you'll recognize it after looking at the illustrations here.

Liverpool ware was the first to be decorated with transfer printing. Before John Sadler and Guy Green discovered how to transfer a print to pottery instead of to paper, all pottery had been decorated exclusively by hand. The transfer-print process introduced a new method that gave the world not only

195. Liverpool pitchers are favorites of collectors, for each one tells a story of old sailing days. *Robert Bourgeault Antiques*

ship pictures on pottery but pictures of many other things. It resulted finally in a commercial rather than an artistic product.

Sadler and Green discovered that they needed only a press, a little soap, and the color they wished to use, to make a print. The ship painting was engraved, then transferred to very thin paper, which was wrapped around the clay body. Thus, the picture was transferred quickly to the pottery.

Liverpool punch bowls were decorated inside and out. Usually there was a tribute to an event or a notable: "Safe Journey to America," or "Congratulations" to whatever ship and captain were being honored. Many occasions called for an inscription—when a ship sailed from port or when a captain had a new command. I saw one of these bowls for sale at an antiques show for five hundred dollars, a figure that would have astonished the enterprising Liverpool potters. Pitchers were more common than punch bowls, and varied widely in the amount and intricacy of decoration. Prices on these begin at around one hundred dollars.

Other Staffordshire potters also made wares with ships as decorations. Wedgwood was the outstanding exporter. His pottery was known in both Europe and America in the eighteenth century. In the intervening two hundred years, a number of Wedgwood plates have been made using ships as decoration. Some are in blue and white, some in black and cream. Wedgwood, too, made punch bowls with ships and inscriptions as the decoration.

196. This blue Staffordshire pitcher was made about 1824 to commemorate the opening of the section of the Erie Canal between Utica and Rochester. The inscription, in praise of the growth of Utica, says that in thirty years this village, "inferior to none in the western section of the state," has grown from a wilderness. On the reverse side is an inscription praising the state and Governor De Witt Clinton. The border decoration depicts canalboats and locks. *Courtesy of The Antique Trader*

197. Old blue and white Delft is not easily found today, but those pieces that do come to light are often decorated with ship paintings typical of this Dutch-made ware. These vases were found in the Hudson River Valley area.

198. From the sixteenth through the nineteenth century, the Dutch Delft potteries were famous for representations of ships in blue and white. You can distinguish the earlier ones exported to this country from those made toward the end of the nineteenth century because the earlier ones had a softer clay body and even look more porous. *Hilbert Brothers Collection*

199. A plate made to commemorate Commodore Perry by one of the Staffordshire potters. *John Bihler & Henry Coger Antiques*

200. Staffordshire platter, black transfer decorated, from the Picturesque Views series. The scene is of the Village of Hudson, on the Hudson River. This series, made by Clews, dates from the first quarter of the nineteenth century. *Pinney Collection*

201. A Staffordshire plate by Mason. In view of the poetic license permitted early decorators, possibly the small steam stack amidship is turned at right angles in disguised tribute to the *Savannah. Rita Merdinger*

202. A plate from a modern Wedgwood series showing historic Canadian vessels. The *Tilikum,* depicted here, was originally a dugout canoe from the Northwest, carved from a cedar log. It was rigged and transformed into a seaworthy vessel. Captain John C. Voss sailed her on a 40,000-mile voyage. This series of Wedgwood plates (see also Illustrations 203, 204, and 205), though fairly recent, bears superb representations of the early Canadian vessels.

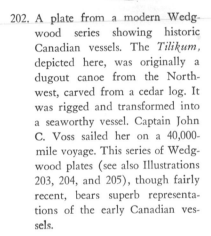

Of particular interest to Americans is a series of more recent Wedgwood plates showing the early vessels of Canada (Ills. 202 through 205). These ships are a part of our heritage, too, having sailed on the lakes and rivers our countries share in common.

Little of the earlier American pottery survives; most that is available is from the nineteenth century. (Before that, pottery was largely imported from abroad.) There is small doubt that at least a few of the early stoneware jugs and crocks made in this country were decorated with nautical motifs. The Henry Ford Museum in Dearborn, Michigan, has a fine example of such a jug bearing a full-rigged sailing ship. An early New Jersey firm, the Salamander (Pottery) Works of Woodbridge, produced an earthenware pitcher with Rockingham-brown glaze depicting a steamship with both smokestack and sails; the Brooklyn Museum too has an outstanding specimen. But finds like these are not only uncommon; they command a high price.

Waiting to be found and identified—if somewhere it rests—is a plate we know to have been issued at the time of Judge Marshall's famous decision that

203. The *York,* an example of a type of boat developed in Canada for carrying cargoes on the inland rivers, was also portrayed in the modern Wedgwood series. Not cargo alone but people traveled on vessels of every kind on our inland lakes and rivers. An excursion on a steamship was the peak attraction.

204. Wedgwood's modern commemorative plate series shows *H.M.S. St. Lawrence,* the largest vessel in tonnage ever to sail the Great Lakes. She was dismantled at Kingston, and relics from her may be seen at the Museum at Old Fort Henry.

205. The *Nonsuch* too is depicted in the modern Wedgwood historical plate series. With a tonnage of forty-three, and an overall length of fifty-five feet, she sailed from England in 1668, in search of the elusive Northwest Passage. She reached the very bottom of Hudson Bay, established Fort Charles, and wintered there with her crew, though the earth "looked like a frozen carcus." Pottery and porcelain portraying historic events, even if not antique themselves, appeal to nautical collectors.

A

206 A. & B. The old Wedgwood plate (*A*) is decorated with a transfer print of the Derby wharf in Salem, Massachusetts. From here the ships of Elias Hasket Derby took off for the Far East, whence they returned with bulging, wealth-producing cargoes. All told, Derby's ship made 125 voyages around the dangerous waters of the Horn to the mysterious Orient—and only *one* of his vessels was lost. The other plate (*B*) depicts Nantucket in the days when whalers were going in and out of her ports. *John Bihler & Henry Coger Antiques*

B

broke the Fulton-Livingston monopoly controlling, for steamboats, the waters of the Hudson. Judge Marshall held that it did not matter whether the vessel was propelled "by wind or by fire," thus ending not only the Hudson River monopoly but others existing in the waters around Philadelphia and in rivers and lakes everywhere. The decision made the waters of the United States free to steamship travel as well as sail. The plate issued in commemoration bore the words, "By wind or by fire." Examples must exist, waiting only for discovery and identification.

During the late nineteenth and early twentieth centuries, commemorative plates became as great a fad as souvenir spoons. Many companies made them. Lenox China, for example, has a particularly interesting commemorative series: on individual plates are pictured each of the yachts that won the America's Cup Race (Ill. 208).

The Buffalo Pottery also used ships as decoration. On its rare Abino ware, small sailing vessels, harbor scenes, and lighthouses often appear. At the time that we started Longacres Riding Camp in western New York, Bill Bown, president of Buffalo Pottery, brought over bushel baskets of the pottery's commercial ware, once made for shipping lines and other companies. Some of it bore ships as decoration. Unfortunately, that pottery has now vanished—replaced with matched sets as the camp outgrew these miscellaneous place settings.

One especially desirable piece of Buffalo Pottery is a 1907 souvenir pitcher of New Bedford, Massachusetts, decorated in brown with a whaling scene, anchor, and the whaleship *Niger*. Two other Buffalo Pottery pitchers with nautical scenes, both dated 1906, are decorated in blue. One shows sailors, a ship, and a lighthouse; the other bears a lightship and various sailing vessels. Buffalo's John Paul Jones pitcher, dated 1907, is decorated in blue not only with the naval hero himself in full figure but a battle scene showing his ship, the *Bonhomme Rich-*

207. Buffalo Pottery offers a rich field for nautical collectors. Almost all the Abino ware made by the company had ships or lighthouses as decoration. This mug, an experimental piece that led to the making of the famous Deldare ware, is an example. *Karl and Gladys Kranz Collection*

208. The Lenox China plate shown here was designed in the early 1900s by Frank Holmes, one of the firm's designers. It is decorated with a sepia decal print made at Trenton using copper plates. The vessel is the yacht *Mayflower*. *Courtesy of Lenox China*

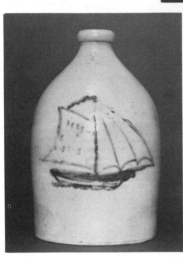

209. American stoneware jug, two-gallon capacity, impressed "N. CLARK Jr./Athens, N.Y.," with rare cobalt-blue slip decoration depicting a Hudson Valley sloop, circa 1860. *Collection of Mr. and Mrs. Barry Shatoff*

ard. All these pitchers—or jugs, as they are usually termed—sell today for $150 and more. (Incidentally, Buffalo Pottery made an advertising plate in 1910 that bears a view of the locks on the Erie Canal at Lockport, New York; another advertising plate made by the pottery depicts Buffalo's Jack Knife Bridge in an open position with a vessel entering the harbor.)

Scuba divers continually bring up shards of pottery from wrecks—and sometimes the prize of a complete dish. That is the hard way to come by a pottery treasure from the sea, or of the sea. The top shelf of your own cupboard may be an easier, and even more productive, source of a great find (see Ill. 11).

ENGRAVED COMMEMORATIVE GLASS

It is harder to find pieces of American commemorative glass than to find commemorative pottery. For one thing, English potteries made many pieces commemorating American ships and captains. From the dearth of surviving glass it would seem that English glass factories did not follow the potters' custom, but perhaps concentrated on the naval events of their own land.

The examples we have of commemorative glass point to the goblet as the accepted form. It usually carried a legend around the rim, followed by the ship's name: "Success to Privateer," for example, with a picture of the ship on the bowl of the goblet. Decanters also were engraved with ships. Generally these are English, but there may be a considerable number of American-made issues that have not been found.

210. Stained-glass panel from the saloon of the elegant Columbia River side-wheel steamer *T. J. Potter*. Windows of stained glass were used in the stern of Spanish vessels for decoration in the sixteenth century. This panel is commemorative of an old custom, and interesting in itself. *Columbia River Maritime Museum*

211. Etched glass hides its full beauty in most photographs, as it does in this photograph of a glass portrait of an early packet, the first built by the Nelson line. *Charles B. Smith*

A Pittsburgh glass factory made a covered goblet with a tribute to the U.S.S. sloop-of-war *Kearsarge* engraved on both sides. The engraving shows the triumph of the *Kearsarge* over the *Alabama*. This was a victory that seemed almost incredible to the North. At the time, the story was portrayed in pictures, song, and story as well as on glass. Under the daring command of Captain Ralph Semmes, the *Alabama* had practically destroyed the shipping of the North—in eleven months, Captain Semmes had captured sixty-nine Union ships and forced the rest of the navy to run for cover. The *Kearsarge* finally cornered the *Alabama* in Cherbourg harbor. Coming out to do battle, the *Alabama* was forced to strike her colors in less than two hours. The news sped across the Atlantic. A victory long dreamed of, and thought impossible, had been won.

Under such circumstances, it seems more than likely that the event would have been widely commemorated in glass. Indeed, I have seen a second proof of this in a goblet displayed in the booth of Valdemar Jacobsen at the New York Coliseum Antiques Show. Two such unusual commemoratives point to others. You may be fortunate enough to find one.

Time has taken its toll of so fragile a medium as glass. Sometimes a shipbuilder commissioned a glass cutter to engrave the new ship's likeness on glass. Examples I have seen are on framed panels, rather than on table glass, as was the English custom. But truly fine table glass was made in America, and ships were so universally admired that it is quite possible examples are hiding somewhere in kitchen cupboards.

COMMEMORATIVE PRESSED GLASS

Pressed glass is rarely thought of as commemorative of our early ships, but there are enough such pieces to whet the desire of any nautical collector. Pressed pitchers, goblets, platters, plates, designed in many and varied patterns, are eagerly sought. The collecting of sets is almost a national pastime. Nautical commemoratives, however, are not found in these sets, but in the earlier cup plates and lacy boat salts. There are not so many, but they make an interesting addition to any collection.

Cup plates were delicate little plates about three inches in diameter that, in the days when drinking tea first became quite common, were used to hold the teacups while the hot beverage cooled in the saucers or was even sipped from them. They were regarded as a popular necessity from about 1827 to 1852 or so. Moreover, they were among the early glass made by Deming Jarves's Sandwich Glass Company—it was he who introduced the process of pressing glass in this country. Three cup plates could be pressed at a time in his machine. The design of the cup plate was engraved on the plunger that fit into the cylinder; it was transferred to the molten glass in the bottom.

Deming Jarves quite changed the process of glassmaking in this country. It is interesting that the development came in the same period of time when aquatints, wood engravings, and lithographs were just catching the imagination of the American people. Personally, I have never noticed a pressed glass cup plate in any maritime museum, although their walls are covered with prints in the other mediums.

The Boston and Sandwich Glass Company that Jarves established made a number of historical nautical cup plates. Excavations on the site of the old factory by researchers from the Massachusetts Institute of Technology turned up fragments of these commemorative little plates in both clear and colored glass. The Sandwich factory, however, was not the only one to make them. There were a number of glass factories in the "Midwest" (the term at that time applied to western Pennsylvania, West Virginia, Ohio, and Indiana) that made some cup plates too, but it would seem that any they made bearing ships were copied from the Sandwich output. These different versions of a pattern of decoration are known as "variants." The *Constitution*, for example, appears on a number of slightly varying cup plates; the one made at Sandwich has a scalloped edge, but an octagon-shaped plate depicting the *Constitution* is known to have been made by a Pittsburgh glass factory.

Both were apparently made at the time that Oliver Wendell Holmes's poem "Old Ironsides" so roused the public that the government, in 1830, rescinded its plans to scrap the old frigate.

One hundred years later, when the *Constitution* was rebuilt again, Gordon Grant made some etchings that are collectors' prizes today. School children all over the country sent pennies to help their government in the expense. To the many who contributed, we who have pride in the oldest warship afloat are grateful.

All told, five fragments of cup plates bearing ships were found in diggings at Sandwich. The earliest is believed to picture the *Chancellor Livingston*, the first steamship to have a regular run on Long Island Sound. She went from New York to Providence on a scheduled run until 1834, quite an achievement for a steamer of that day.

Steamers were a marvelous invention to the people of the early nineteenth century. Paintings, prints, and cup plates bearing their likenesses were always popular. The only Sandwich cup plate to feature a clipper showed the *Cadmus*, the ship that brought General Lafayette to the United States for his triumphal tour. The *Cadmus* also appears on other pieces of pressed glass—an early compote bears its image, and it is on a round lacy salt from Sandwich. The ship is depicted in alternate medallions around the salt, the other medallions containing the American eagle.

The *Benjamin Franklin*, another early steamer, is found on Sandwich cup plates (Ill. 212). With her sister ship the *William Penn*, she initiated regular passenger travel between Boston and Philadelphia. The two steamers sailed from alternate ports every other Saturday, but the *Benjamin Franklin* was the one chosen to be commemorated in glass. Otherwise it might have been completely forgotten, for the Philadelphia and Boston Packet Line, as the owners called the two steamers, failed to prosper. It was in operation for less than a year, from 1851 to some time in 1852. Then, aside from a specially advertised trip, the two little steamers were not heard from again. They were sold abroad, the *Benjamin Franklin* to Venezuela in 1856.

212. Sandwich glass cup plate showing the packet *Benjamin Franklin,* one of the few illustrations of this vessel. This cup plate, like a number of others, has been reproduced, but not recently. *Pinney Collection*

The last of the five Sandwich ship cup plates, the *Maid-of-the-Mist*, was almost a grace note at the end of the cup plate era, around 1857. The *Maid-of-the-Mist*, which carried Niagara Falls sightseers to the base of the falls on the turbulent waters of the Niagara, was a favorite of travelers. Today, another steamer performs the same service, but she is shorn of the reverent glory that clung to the first *Maid-of-the-Mist*.

The early cup plates were often uneven in appearance, especially if the plunger on which the ship was engraved did not descend evenly. Also, the mold might not fill evenly with glass. Sometimes there were hairlines or little surface ruptures. About 1836, when more heat was being used to keep the glass molten, the surface was sometimes blurred. These little technical blemishes are important to remember, for cup plates have been reproduced as their prices have risen. However, many more cup plates were made that were perfect than that had blemishes.

When cup plates were no longer popular, pressed glass was used to commemorate historical events, among them the exploits of the Spanish-American War heroes, Admiral George Dewey and his flagship captain, Charles Gridley. One example on record is amply documented as follows: A glass pitcher about nine inches high bears the likeness of the then Commodore Dewey; a scroll with the names *Olympia, Petrel, Concord, Raleigh, Boston,* and *Baltimore* (the ships at the scene of the Battle of Manila Bay); the American flag beside the inscription "Gridley, you may fire when ready"; a sailor holding a flag with four stars; and—just to be sure there was no mistake about this illustrious occasion—the inscription "Manila, May 1st, 1898."

In pressed glass there are other reminders of the sea—for example, the famed dolphins that were used in candlesticks and to serve as standards for compotes. And in pressed glass dinner sets there are shell patterns of interest to some nautical collectors, but these scarcely come under the heading of commemorative pieces, pleasant as they are to find and to own. Ships were used in many ways on pressed glass in the days when it was popular. The Corning Museum of Glass has a number of examples in its extensive exhibition—for example, a glass boat flower stand made by the English firm of Stevens and Williams. This eighteen-inch container for flowers is in the form of a boat, which rests on a stand of glass rods fused together. It dates from about 1885.

COMMEMORATIVE SILVER

Silver teapots, bowls, and cups were considered the most desirable of any commemorative pieces in the eighteenth and nineteenth centuries. Not only was silver a precious metal, but such articles were hand-wrought and hand-engraved. These commemorative pieces are usually seen in museums or as prized possessions of the descendants of those to whom they were given. The design of the pieces varies, but often they bear an engraving of the ship, the date, and an inscription in the beautiful cursive engraving of the period—perhaps to the master taking over a new veessel, or expressing good wishes for a successful journey to the Orient. Some pieces commemorate the winning of a race.

Sometimes old silver cups and bowls have not been cherished. I saw a commemorative bowl with a toast to DeWitt Clinton on one side and, on the other, an engraving of the city of Buffalo at the time of the opening of the Erie Canal. It was found in an antiques shop. Because, over a long period, silver will tarnish until it is nearly black, good pieces are often discarded by the families who originally owned them. A discerning collector can sometimes pick them up cheap, and with polish, labor, and research elevate them to a well-deserved place in his collection.

Flat silver occasionally offers collectors of nautical antiques a special prize, but it is rare. This is strange, since the luxury liners of the 1890s and early 1900s are credited with being instrumental in popularizing the use of flat silver. Various ships featured silver from certain specific silver companies, and this meant so much to the silver-manufacturing firms that a successful bid was news. Special silver patterns were featured on each ship, and what was more natural than that the passengers would want to own the very pattern they had so admired on shipboard? What an excellent means for boasting of one's travels!

The importance of such orders is illustrated by an announcement in the *Jeweler's Circular Weekly*, May 21, 1900, that eight new American liners of the International Navigation Company's fleet were to be furnished with the silver patterns of the Holmes and Edwards Silver Company (later taken over by the International Silver Company). The eight ships were to be equipped with inlaid sets of silver similar to sets that had proved so popular on two earlier vessels of the International Navigation Company.

Noel D. Turner reprinted notices like this in his book *American Silver Flatware.** But though luxury liners popularized flat silver, as did hotels and railroads, they did not appear to buy silver that featured patterns from the sea. In flat-silver patterns from 1837 to 1910, the only ones that really spoke of the sea were the shell patterns. Some dozen or more firms used a version of the shell pattern on their flatware. In all of them there was a shell in relief at the top of the handle. Sometimes this was the only decoration. At other times various types of Victorian scrolls surrounded it. But the patterns are not so different that they could not be used together in a silver service. A nautical collector I know has assembled such a set of flat silver and uses it with particular pride.

Occasionally one finds ship motifs on the souvenir spoons that were so popular seventy or more years ago. Sometimes pictures of ships were inscribed

---

* South Brunswick, N.J., and New York: A. S. Barnes, 1972.

in the bowl, but it would almost seem that buyers of souvenir spoons in the nineties considered ships much too commonplace, preferring buildings and names and places. It is hard to believe that there are not more ships on souvenir spoons. They may be rare, but they must be there—the manufacturers of silver spoons for souvenirs appear to have omitted almost no subject. Moreover, every silver spoon manufacturer had a line of blanks, spoons completely finished by the manufacturer except for the bowl, so that with the help of a good engraver even remote villages and lonely sea towns could have their souvenir spoon. You may find one.

WHALING COLLECTIONS

Whaling, which was one of the first great American industries, has left behind not nearly enough historic relics to satisfy those who collect them. Not only was whaling colorful, exciting, and often dangerous, but its story is purely American. Almost all other industries that offer collectible treasures stem from a European background.

Not that whaling began in America—Basque fishermen, in the tenth century, made it a pursuit. Whaling was practiced by all the coastal countries. The occasional narwhal tusk the fishermen brought back probably gave rise, historians say, to stories of the unicorn—that fabulous animal with one horn. The narwhal had a single long spiral tusk extending from its upper jaw.

With the emergence of the United States as a nation, the "Empire of the Quakers" began, and America became the acknowledged center and leader of the whaling trade. Quaker promoters amassed unbelievable wealth as they went north to the Arctic, south to the Antarctic, west to Hawaii, and along the coasts of Chile and Peru in their search for whales. The industry was centered in the area around Long Island Sound and up the coast of Massachusetts to New Bedford, which became the leader, and Nantucket. Closely following New Bedford in importance were Bristol, Newport, and Warren in Rhode Island, Sag Harbor on Long Island, and Stonington and New London in Connecticut. Whalers even set out from the little New York State village of Hudson, some one hundred miles up the Hudson River from the coast!

It was 1791 when American whaling vessels first entered the Pacific. Only five were involved in this first adventure. In 1792, three American whalers rounded the Horn. By the peak year of 1846, there were something more than seven hundred United States whalers, not all of which went to the Pacific. It was a life predicated less on the high adventure with which we endow it in our twentieth-century imagination than on the pursuit of a sound and lucrative career.

The sperm whale, the right whale, and the bowhead or Greenland whale

213. The *Joseph Conrad,* one of
the few sailing vessels that
can be found today, lies at
Mystic Seaport, Mystic,
Connecticut. *Photograph
by Edward W. Vidler*

were the ones that could be caught. So, too, to a lesser extent could the hump-back and California gray. Other species, such as the blue and the finback, the whalers could not catch because these whales could swim too fast and sound too deep, or they sank when killed.

All these factors have combined in the mind of today's American collec-tors to make whaling relics—indeed, all the artifacts and almost every reminder from those days—very expensive. This has given an added value to whaling prints. Not so many of them were made, and those that were made have been picked up whenever found. It makes listing even the great ones scarcely neces-sary. They can be seen in museums and read about in some excellent books. Most of them illustrate the dramatic side of whaling: small boats being nearly crushed or overturned by the great mammal. The capture of the whales and the activi-ties of the men seeking them can all be found in prints, engravings, lithographs, wood engravings, aquatints. If you happen to come upon one for a price you can afford, you will not go wrong in buying it, for interest in whaling is not decreasing. It seems to be going up and up, with collectors advertising for any-thing connected with whaling.

We have already spoken of scrimshaw, the one truly American folk art. It is the principal item in a large number of collections, but it too is rare and scarce.

There is also a wide interest in any tools connected with the industry. Sev-eral museums have on display the kettles in which the blubber was "tried out" to make the whale oil. And there are the tools used in taking the whale—har-poons, harpoon guns, bomb lances, and so on. A harpoon, if you're interested, is very expensive in dealers' shops. Unusual ones or those with refinements on them cost still more.

In addition to whaling prints, there were scrolls—lengths of cloth on which whaling pictures were painted. Unrolled, they were exhibited to the public. Some of them were absolutely monumental. There is a scroll in New Bedford that was painted in 1848 by two men, Purrington and Russell (Benjamin Rus-sell came from a family that owned a whaling fleet). The 650-foot-long scroll illustrates episodes in Herman Melville's *Moby-Dick*, the classic saga of whales and men, as fascinating today as when it was written.

Scrolls, however rare, can be found. I say this because I found one (Ill. 214). I couldn't believe it then; it still seems incredible today. I was in a thrift shop, and looking over toward the picture gallery I saw what I thought was a framed newspaper print of whaling scenes. Nonetheless, I sped across the three aisles to examine it and discovered that it was not a newspaper but a handwoven linen scroll on which, in dramatic fashion, Yankee whaling had been portrayed. It touched me, too, that it began with a thought of home—the widow's walk, where two women looked out to sea waiting, waiting for that whaler to come home.

214. Sailing scrolls are rare, but they provide tangible descriptions of a way of life that is gone. ❯
    Here, Yankee whaling scenes were drawn with India ink on homespun cloth and signed
    by the artist. (See the separate photographs of the individual scenes.)

YANKEE WHALING

From the roofs, wives watched for their husbands' ships.

Sperm oil of the highest grade was bailed from the tank in the whale's head.

Using lance for the final kill.

The blubber was carved into blocks, called "horse pieces."

The Right Whale

The Sperm Whale

Harpoon

A sperm whale turns on its hunters.

by Warren Baucher

It is experiences like this that make nautical collectors. You may not know where the "whales" are, but interest and knowledge can help in their capture.

215. Significantly, the artist began his scroll with what is called the widow's walk, an architectural feature of captains' houses in practically all the early seaports. From such a railed platform on the roof a wife watched for her husband's ship. At right, the artist showed "Sperm oil of the highest grade" being bailed from the whale's head. Drawings of the whalers' activities are prized because they clarify the use of tools and show how the operation was carried out.

216. "Using lance for the final kill"—and considerable courage, too.

After all, ours is a more humane approach. In fact, it would seem but right that all of us who enjoy stories and tales of the yesteryear of whaling should unite to protect the whale, which is in serious danger of extinction.

217. "The blubber was carved into blocks, called 'horse pieces.'"

218. "A sperm whale turns on its hunters": the horror that haunted every whaler.

THE CHINA EXPORT TRADE

From 1785, when the *Empress of China* sailed into the port of New York from her successful journey to Canton and back, with Chinese porcelain packed in her hold, until 1972, when a piece sold at auction at Sotheby Parke-Bernet for $20,000, this translucent ware has been loved by collectors. There is no doubt that it will continue to be.

To those who have come under the spell of Chinese porcelain, into each piece are fired history, romance, and a bit of magic. To our forefathers, these dishes, through which one could see light—they gave them the name of "china" —were so coveted that they ranked highest among the many treasures that came from the land of spice. To us they speak of wooden sailing ships and mighty men who, with their small vessels and the most elementary navigational guides, made the perilous journey around the Horn and on to China.

These voyages were tremendous achievements, but not without their rich reward in gold, not without the appreciation of one's peers. The New York *Packet*, on May 12, 1785, recorded the return of the *Empress of China,* the first American ship to make the run, in these words:

> We have the satisfaction of announcing the arrival of the Ship *Empress of China,* Capt. Greene, Commander, from the East Indies, at this port, yesterday, after a voyage of fourteen months and twenty-four days. She sailed from this port about the 15th of February, 1784. . . . We learn that Captain Greene met with polite usage during his stay in Canton. The British Commodore was the first who saluted his flag on his arrival there. Some years ago when the advantages of trade and navigation were better studied and more valued than they are now, the arrival of a vessel after so prosperous a voyage, from so distant a part of our globe would be an-

nounced by public thanksgiving and ringing of bells!—Should not this be our practice now, since Providence is countenancing our navigation to this world? We hope in our next to give our readers a more perfect detail of this important voyage.

And, in their "next," the news is of the aromatic root, ginseng:

Among the many other articles sent from our Port to China in this ship (*Empress of China*) was a considerable quantity of the root Ginseng. . . . The government of China sends 10,000 Tartar soldiers every year to gather this plant, and each is obliged to bring home two ounces of the best Ginseng gratis, and for the rest they are paid its weight in silver. Private persons are not allowed to gather it, but this odious prohibition does not prevent them.

A better idea of some of these porcelains from China is given in advertisements that appeared some ten years later. Delannoy and Goynard, 119 Pearl Street, advertised a shipment of "blue and white and painted china in table and tea sets, Bowls, Cups, and Saucers, and East India table cloths." In Argus Greenleaf's *New Daily Advertiser*, August 9, 1796, and William Laight and Co. in the *Independent Journal or the General Advertiser* "Have for Sale China Ware, pencilled in Gilt, Imported in the *Experiment*, Capt. Dean just arrived from China, May 2, 1797."

The fullest description of this early China ware that I have come across was given by Maria S. Morton in the *New York Gazette and County Journal*, June 14, 1785, who advertised she had on hand:

China arrived from Canton in the Ship *Empress of China* Table and Tea

219. Oil painting on canvas, mid-nineteenth century, of Canton, China; Chinnery school. Canton and the Pearl River estuary were familiar territory to American sailing ships from 1800 on. *Mystic Seaport photograph, Mystic, Connecticut*

Setts compleat. Blue and white and enamelled half pint basons and saucers, Blue and white and enamelled Breakfast and common cups and saucers. Blue and white and enamelled and bowls of different sizes. Two very curious small Tea Chests. All will be sold low. Jersey currency taken as payment.

220. This example of exquisite workmanship shows the beauty of Japanese design on porcelain. Punch bowls were a favored item to bring from the Orient in the eighteenth and nineteenth centuries.

221. Glass is so fragile that few very early pieces are found. Yet, within a year, two reverse paintings on glass of Washington were discovered, drawn in the early 1800s from the same original print sent to Canton to be copied for Americans. Some three hundred of these rare paintings on glass have been found with identifiable Chinese touches. *John Bihler & Henry Coger Antiques*

222. Chinese export ware was one of the most sought after of the wares brought here in a clipper's hold. Punch bowls were highly prized, nor have they lost their appeal today. One such as this was recently advertised for $3800.

The first Chinese porcelains to be imported were pieces that had been made in China for use at home, but by the seventeenth century porcelain-making had been expanded to create articles for foreign trade. Among the early promoters were the French Jesuit fathers. Père d'Entrecolles's name comes down to us because of two letters he wrote describing the making of the "new" substance. He had the potters in Ching-te-chen, the great porcelain manufacturing city, create porcelains with religious motifs. Biblical and crucifixion scenes, sometimes combined with Buddhist symbols, appear on plates and even tea sets in blue and white.

The most popular china in both the European and American markets, however, was heraldic. Continuing the tradition of silverware decorated with family crests, the patrons of the new medium demanded crests on their porcelains. These armorial bearings sometimes enable one to date a piece of porcelain within a few years of its origin.

Punch bowls followed tea sets in popularity (Ill. 222). Other forms were candlesticks, cachepots (to hold flowerpots), shaving bowls, chamber pots, salt, pepper, and sugar casters. The list is long, and, considering its diversity and volume, it seems that more of these unusual porcelains should be found by collectors today.

223. The translucence of the body, the delicacy of the workmanship, as shown in this close-up of a handle of a Chinese export teapot, made our forefathers feel that this "new substance" from far Cathay was almost magical.

224 A. & B. Silks and embroideries were other trophies of the China trade. Of the two embroideries shown here, the prunus-blossom spray is done on black silk; the royal five-clawed dragon is done in gold thread on red.

225. Carved chessmen and lacquered boards also came here on the clippers.

Collectors refer to one type of this Chinese export porcelain as Lowestoft. That name was applied, originally, to porcelain with a particular floral decoration. Later it was attached to all this ware. However, the name was based on a mistake in a book. None of these Chinese wares were made in the little English town of Lowestoft. Still, the name persists in spite of all efforts to correct the misnomer. So if a dealer says Lowestoft, prick up your ears. If the price is one you can afford, you will not want to pass the item by. In the eighteenth century this porcelain was often called Indian ware because in Europe the East India Company held a monopoly of trade with the East. Call it what you will. Buy it if you can. China export ware is a symbol of a great and colorful era.

7

OF THESE WE DREAM

ALL OVER THE COUNTRY HIDDEN nautical treasures are waiting to be found. This is true in any field of antiques, but especially so in an area just beginning to be popular. In many places, antiques dealers themselves are new to the idea of finding and selling relics from seafaring days. When you ask, they look somewhat puzzled. One said to me: "You mean wheels from ships?"

Marine museums right now are the best source for familiarizing yourself with the possibilities. I am convinced that it is possible to make—and that you will make—discoveries on your own of many rare items. They are waiting for you in the places we have mentioned, and in your own highways and byways.

LOGS AND RECORDS

You may find, for example, a log of a ship's voyage. Every vessel that sailed had its log, a day-by-day account. Some are dryly statistical; others are illustrated accounts that in a few words make a voyage of a hundred years ago come to life. One of the most beautiful examples I have seen is in the Museum of the Massachusetts Institute of Technology in Boston.

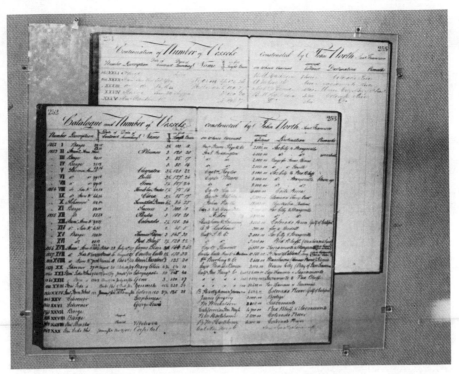

226. Records of business transactions by ships are considered important enough by museums to be put on display. Those kept of expenses on board a ship or schooner, including personal items such as tobacco and soap, provide a flavor of the times. *San Francisco Maritime Museum*

I was once on the trail of a great log. It was not to be mine, but I was going to be able to handle it, to study it—the log of the clipper ship *David Crockett*. My friend Persis Hall, whose relatives had been the owners of the clipper, told me that the log was at the home of her sister, whom she soon would visit; she would bring it back for me to see. It was an exciting moment for a nautical enthusiast, but strange things happen. Unexpectedly, her sister was taken to a nursing home. Various strangers were in the house. The log of the *David Crockett* disappeared.

Other records from old ships are also interesting and valuable. They cast a homely light on the ways of our forefathers. Possibly you have examined some under glass in a museum case and been amazed at the prices paid for commodities and services in the old days. You might be equally surprised at prices if you were to seek to buy an old record from a knowledgeable dealer.

Both the Bath Marine Museum in Maine and the Mystic Seaport Museum in Connecticut have exact replicas of the old counting rooms where ship's officers carried on their business. It's not hard to see the fascination of a receipt that reads, "Receipt for fifty barrels of oil and for tug Harbor."

From surviving examples, we gather that these shipowners were great account keepers, but poor account savers—at least if the few to be found are an indication of their habits. But records of a certainty were kept, for most ships represented big business in their day.

227. This is a stock certificate issued by a shipping line. What is rare is to have one of these certificates survive until today. This one was issued in 1831. *Hilbert Brothers Collection*

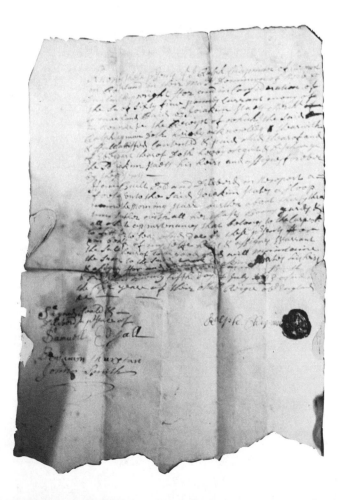

228. These papers specify the contract for a sloop of thirty-three tons to be built. Such records are rare today, especially one like this from 1693. The cost for such a sloop? Sixty-five pounds in "current" money! *Hilbert Brothers Collection*

229. Below the portrait of Captain Burgess is a small poster advertising the *David Crockett* as *the* vessel on which to sail to San Francisco. *Persis Pettis Hall Collection; advertisement reproduced at Mystic Seaport Museum*

230. This lacy-looking ticket served as a passport to the greatest ride in the world—a trip on the Erie Canal. *Picture collection of the New York Public Library*

FLAGS

We don't often picture sailing ships bedecked with flags, but our ancestors felt the same reverence for their vessels as for breathing, sentient beings—they dressed them up with flags. Chinese merchants referred to the ships of Americans as "flowery flagged devils." But the ships of all nations bore flags. One has only to look at the early-eighteenth-century paintings of ships under oar and sail in the Grand Canal of Venice to see what could be achieved with flags. And it was not only Venice; ships arriving in port from any of the European countries were also flag-bedecked in this period, the seventeenth and eighteenth centuries. The Americans, however, flew flags on every mast well through the nineteenth century. There were large American flags, the flag of the ship's owner, and the flag of the ship itself. They were all fragile and easily lost, however, and so it is surprising to see so many in museums.

Probably the most loved were the flags of the shipowners. Tears came to the eyes of the daughter of one of the shipyard owners in Bath, Maine, when she talked of the company's flags. Like royal banners, they stood in a flag holder. The Mallory flags are so displayed in the Mystic Seaport Museum.

The Philadelphia Maritime Museum has a frieze of the colorful flags used by the shippers of that port. The Peabody Museum displays the flags of the

231. No finer time for displaying flags than on launching day! But it was also a tradition of the sea for a vessel to enter port bedecked with all her flags, either proclaiming her safe return or telling whence she hailed. On a three-master, a large American flag hung from the mizzen gaff and the name banner flew from the top of the mainmast. The owner's house flag waved from the foremast. On special occasions also, all the flags would be put up. *Bath Marine Museum*

232. The banner of the *K. V. Kruse*, which flew from the five-masted schooner built by the Kruse and Banks ship-yards. This was the longest banner in the United States to fly from any mast. Only one other vessel had an equally long banner. *Columbia River Maritime Museum*

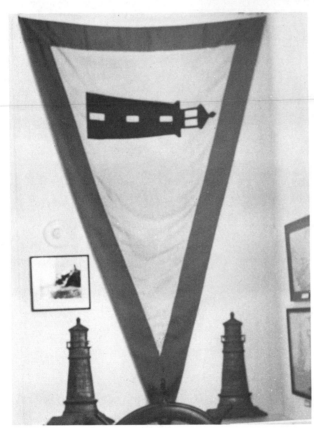

233. The lighthouse pennant was up whenever the keeper was in residence. *Columbia River Maritime Museum*

wealthy merchants of Salem, whose ships went to all parts of the world, in almost royal fashion. And in the Columbia River Maritime Museum is the banner of the *K. V. Kruse* (Ill. 232), a five-masted schooner built by the Kruse and Bank shipyard. Except for one, the *K. V. Kruse* flew the longest banner on the seas.

These emblems were cherished, and some must have escaped destruction, but the only place that I have seen them is on museum walls.

234. These are the flags of Philadelphia merchants—each merchant had a different one. Such flags are now treasured by the city from which the vessels hailed. No ship left port without its house flag flying, but few remain today; the wind tattered them and time has decayed those that survived. *Philadelphia Maritime Museum*

MAPS, GLOBES, AND ATLASES

Consider old maps—the charts by which men found their way in wooden ships across dangerous stretches of water. The best description I have found is the one by Alexander O. Viedter in the *Concise Encyclopedia of American Antiques*. He describes a map as a fascinating hybrid—a cross between a picture and a diagram. You may think you will never find an interesting old map, but not long ago a dealer of my acquaintance had one of Long Island Sound, circa 1840, for sale.

John Foster's map of New England, "the first that was ever cut here," shows the area from Maine to the Connecticut River.

State maps appeared in the first part of the nineteenth century. A friend of mine found a large map of New York State in a one-room schoolhouse that was to be demolished. It was illustrated with state scenes, putting it in the class that

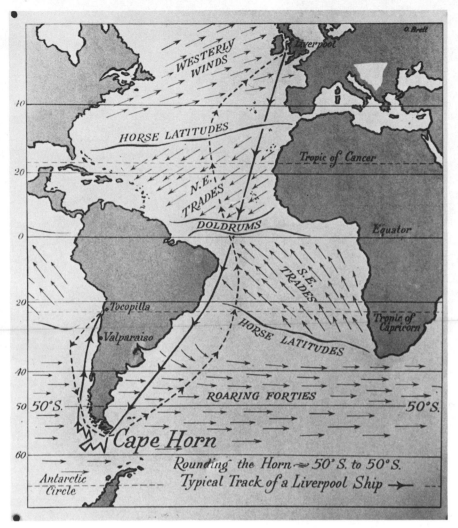

235. Maps like this one showing the "Typical Track of a Liverpool Ship" indicate the difficulties seamen faced in the long voyages they had to endure before the days of the Panama Canal—around the Horn to the Orient or up the west coast of South America. This map is displayed at the South Street Seaport Museum, New York City.

is eagerly sought because of the pictorial angle. Old city maps too were often illustrated with important buildings or scenes, and when the city was a busy seaport, such a map has special significance for the nautical collector (Ills. 236 and 237). These maps are not too difficult to come by today.

The first American globes were made by James Wilson, originally of Bedford, Vermont, and later of Albany, New York. His work is often found in New York, and at comparatively low prices. At about this same time, atlases were first published. County atlases and town plans made their appearance in the second quarter of the nineteenth century. These even show houses and their owners' names. We enjoy studying our Erie County atlas to find the names of captains who sailed the Great Lakes. This intimate knowledge of where they actually lived, perhaps on a street we know in Buffalo, is strangely moving.

Astoria, the only seaport for all classes of ships on the PACIFIC COAST north of San Francisco. Puget Sound cities are from 90 to 150 miles from the Pacific Ocean, while Astoria is only 10 miles distant.

236. Old city and state maps, particularly those illustrated with scenes or pictures of notable buildings, are favorites of collectors, and those of seaports are appropriate in a nautical collection. This illustrated map of Astoria, Oregon, points out that whereas Puget Sound cities are from ninety to a hundred miles from the ocean, Astoria is only ten miles from the Pacific—the only Pacific coast seaport north of San Francisco for all classes of ships! *Columbia River Maritime Museum*

237. This map of New York in 1782 (as surveyed by J. Hills) was republished just over a century later. It shows the New York familiar to arriving vessels in Revolutionary days. Maps of this kind are the ones easiest to find today. *South Street Seaport Museum*

BOOKS, NEWSPAPERS, AND SHEET MUSIC

A closet in my grandfather's home was literally stuffed with old magazines. Floor to ceiling, they were piled—*Century, Harper's Weekly,* and more. He could not bear to let a single back issue go, for fear he might want to look up something, sometime. More practical souls eventually returned this space to coats and hats, and though I was young and had no say in the matter, I would not have known anyway what a cache of nautical interest was stored there. *Harper's Weekly* was filled with wood engravings of ships at sea and contemporary descriptions of battles. There have been reissues, but only the wood engravings from the original magazines are of value.

Old books, intriguing in their own right, take on new luster if you come upon a find in a sea classic—say, Richard Henry Dana's *Two Years Before the Mast,* published in 1840, or *The Seaman's Friend,* 1841, "containing a treatise on practical seamanship, a useful dictionary of sea terms, and valuable information on maritime law."

238. Much of the value in old newspapers is in the wood engravings used for illustrations. Some of the popular ones have been reproduced—for example, *Harper's Weekly* of the Civil War years was reproduced as an educational project. Newspapers, especially those from their home towns, meant a great deal to the men on board ship. Today the engravings of the sea are especially sought. This one depicts the famous yacht *America. Gleason's Pictorial Drawing-Room Companion, 1850*

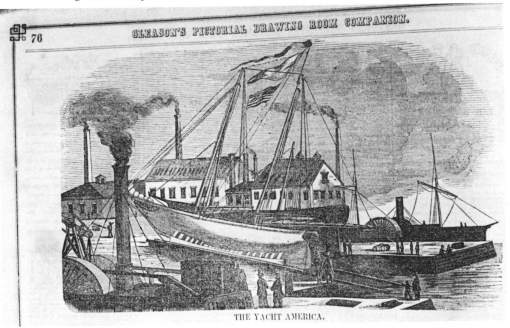

THE YACHT AMERICA.

239 A, B, & C. Rarely does one find intact an entire picture book that was brought home from the Far East by an early ship captain. Even rarer is a picture book from the little-known Philippines. *Hilbert Brothers Collection*

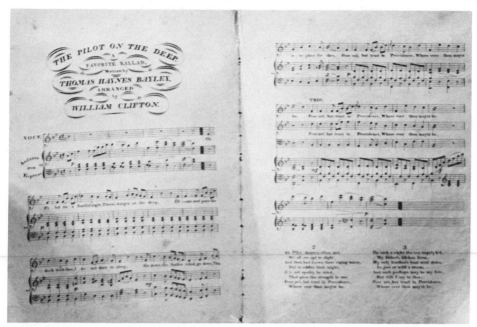

240. Songs were written for the launching of a vessel. Old sheet music of these songs is particularly hard to find. *Orcutt Collection*

241. The covers on old sheet music often have colored illustrations of nautical scenes. *Orcutt Collection*

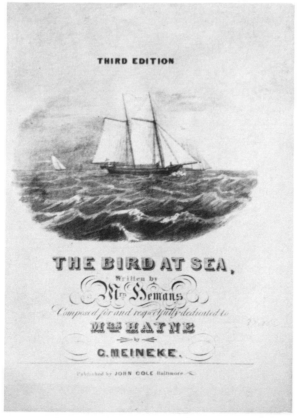

242. Scenes like this one aboard a Gloucester fishing schooner indicate that dancing as well as singing was a popular pastime. In the coastal trade, someone on board ship always had a harmonica or a musical instrument of some sort. On oceangoing vessels, sea chanteys were developed to give a rhythm to work and make it seem lighter. *Gleason's Pictorial Drawing-Room Companion, 1850*

Old songs and sheet music are a minor but delightful field for the nautical collector. Sea chanties call to mind the spirit and stamina of men engaged in a work romantic to our minds, but grueling and dangerous in that day. A researcher of folk songs says that those passed down by sailors to their children and children's children are a rich source of her material.

Here and there you may come upon some seaman's sheet music. It was the custom to compose and dedicate a song to a ship upon its launching, and some of the more important ones were printed. These examples of sheet music are worth searching for—and they *can* be found.

CLIPPER SHIP CARDS

An example of yesterday's ephemera that is today's pure gold for some collectors is the clipper ship card. Like the handbill thrust on us today and tossed into the nearest litter box, the clipper card was handed out in the streets to inform possible passengers of the glory of a particular ship. Then, as now, advertising exploded with superlatives, and speeds beyond the imagination of mid-nineteenth-century travelers were promised for the journey from New York around the Horn to San Francisco.

The pocket-sized cards were lithographed on coated stock in bright colors tinted with gold. Their similarity to trade cards that earlier had been lithographed in Belgium indicates that they may have been the work of Belgian lithographers who had emigrated to Boston and New York in the troubled period of 1848.

I, for one, cannot even find the folder that lured us into a twenty-day Grace Line trip to the West Indies in 1931. Scarcity makes the search grow fonder in the case of items like clipper ship cards. If found, they have been known to sell for as much as two hundred dollars. As is clear from the following example, the promotional excitement of the clipper card's text is charming in itself, even when we cannot see the bright colors.

MERCHANTS' EXPRESS LINE OF CLIPPER SHIPS
FOR
SAN FRANCISCO!

None But A1 Fast Sailing Clippers Loaded In This Line

THE EXTREME CLIPPER SHIP

OCEAN EXPRESS

WATSON, COMMANDER
AT PIER 9, EAST RIVER

This splendid vessel is one of the fastest Clippers afloat, and a great favorite with all shippers. Her commander, Capt. WATSON, was formerly master of the celebrated Clipper "FLYING DRAGON," which made the passage in *97 days*, and of the ship POLYNESIA, which made the passage in *103 days*.

She comes to the berth one third loaded, and has very large engagements.

RANDOLPH M. COOLEY,

118 Water St., cor. Wall, Tontine Building.

Agents in San Francisco, DE WITT, KITTLE & CO.

DEVICES FOR COMMUNICATION

Instant communication is today's commonplace. In the days of sailing ships and early steamships, it sometimes took ingenuity to get the message across. The devices for that purpose are another collecting gift from the sea.

Willard Price, writing in *Decorative Arts of the Mariner*, describes the steam calliopes used on Mississippi steamboats in the early 1900s. Among such boats was the *Avalon*, whose organ sent up a series of whistles when the keys were pressed. It took muscle to play a tune, but everyone for a half-mile along the river knew that the *Avalon* was on its way!

Bells were used in many ways on shipboard—to enable the captain to communicate with the engine room, for announcing the watch, and so on. One that has come down in the Russell Haley family was used on several schooners in Long Island Sound. It looks more like an old school bell than a seagoing one, but it does make a mighty clang when the clapper strikes the brass sides. Around 1850, one of the wonders of the luxury riverboats was the installation of a bell system in the cabins enabling the passengers to summon the steward.

Bells, along with the more familiar foghorn and steam whistle, were also used to signal fog. Gongs, it is said, could be heard no farther than a quarter of a mile. Bells did better in a fog, being audible at a distance of one to three

243. Bells were used on shipboard for many purposes. They can be found today in a varied assortment of sizes. This one was used on board a naval vessel. *Columbia River Maritime Museum*

245. Every ship carried hailing trumpets, precursors of the modern megaphone. These examples are typical. *Bath Marine Museum*

244. This small handbell—exactly like those used by generations of old-time schoolmasters—is from the *W. E. and W. L. Tuck,* a coastal schooner.

246. One method of signaling from one ship to another is illustrated in this early wood engraving. *Harper's Weekly 1861*

247. A naval signal-flare pistol could be of vital importance on board ship. *Nina Hellman Antiques*

miles. Guns were used too, and they could be heard, with a light breeze blowing, at a ten-mile distance. But most powerful of all was the foghorn, which under favorable circumstances was heard from twenty to thirty miles out at sea.

A system for signaling by flag at sea was devised by Sir Home Popham in 1803, Captain Marryat in 1817, and others. A collector deciding to investigate this field, with its international code and the changes and revisions through the years, needs to be scholarly as well as persistent.

TOOLS OF THE TRADE

Each craft connected with shipbuilding had its tools. Examples are collected and displayed by museums—for the excellence of their construction as well as for the information they give about the early industry. We have a pair of foresighted collectors to thank for one of the most complete exhibits of early tools in this country. Long before others were interested in preserving this part of the past, Henry K. and George D. Landis began to assemble old tools and devices. That was in 1880. Their work was so comprehensive that the state of Pennsylvania has now housed the collection in a separate museum, a real source of reference for tool lovers—the Landis Valley Museum at Lancaster, Pennsylvania.

Less extensive collections of tools are given prominence in many maritime museums. Even small displays occupy a considerable space if they properly tell the story, for many crafts were involved in building a vessel, and inevitably there was carpentering to be done aboard ship during her voyages.

Recognizing that few people are privileged to be present at a ship launching, the Bath Marine Museum exhibits the ways down which a ship slid into the sea, and models of accessories to the launching.

248. This unusually interesting and detailed white-line engraving from *A Pictorial Encyclopedia* (Trades and Industries), by Denis Diderot, illustrates many of the tools and techniques used in shipbuilding. *Courtesy of Dover Publications, 1959, Plate 290*

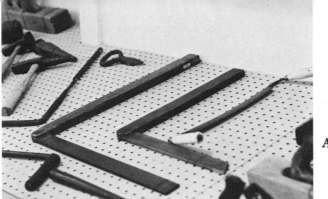

A

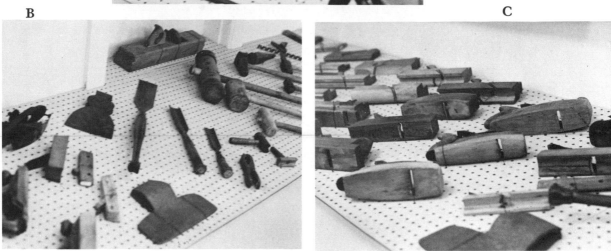

B

C

249 A, B, & C. The Columbia River Maritime Museum has a fine display of old shipbuilding tools. The two early squares (*A*) are made of wood; the drawknife has handles of painted wood. There are caulkers' mallets and a large one used to pound in treenails (*B*), as well as gouges of various sizes. The long-handled flat chisel next to the broadaxe head is known as a slick; it smoothed the wood after the broadaxe had done its work. There are no duplicates in the collection of planes (*C*)—each had its specific purpose.

250. The wood sculptor too had his special tools, including some he made himself to answer the needs of a particular task. *Orcutt Collection*

251. Eel spears, used in Colonial days. *Nina Hellman Antiques*

TOYS AND GAMES

Throughout history, children's playthings have mimicked the tools and favorite articles of their parents' world. Even grownups feel pleasure in a well-made replica of some prosaic houeshold object—a hand-painted tea set, a tiny doll's trunk complete with trays and compartments. Just as little girls used to play with "sad irons" and toy stoves, little boys inevitably coveted and owned fire engines, sailboats, and steamships. Naturally these trivia of bygone days—worn out, or outgrown and carelessly thrown away—have come into their own as things to collect, made desirable by their scarcity as well as their charm.

I well remember a carefully made model of the ferryboat that plied its way between Buffalo, New York, and Fort Erie in Canada. One of the joys of our children's childhood was to take the three-foot model of the ferryboat to Fort Erie, compare it with the boat on which they sailed, and then float it in the waters of the lake. None of us can remember what became of it.

Of the toy ships made especially for children many years ago, too few survive and those that do are collectors' finds indeed. Indians used to sell authentic birchbark canoe models on the streets of Buffalo, another source of delight to our children, who saved their pennies to acquire full fleets of them. But where, oh, where, are these formerly treasured articles now? One I recall in particular as a small masterpiece. With hindsight I wonder: "Why did I let the children have it for a plaything?"

Yet experience proves that, for the looking, toys made for the sea and its ways can be found—from the early twentieth century, the nineteenth century, and even a few from the eighteenth century. Most of those that have been preserved are either boats or dolls. In a museum I saw a fine old doll dressed in the costume of a French sailor of the eighteenth century, with a round pomponned

252. Toy boats of tin. *Patricia and Sanford Smith Galleries, New York City*

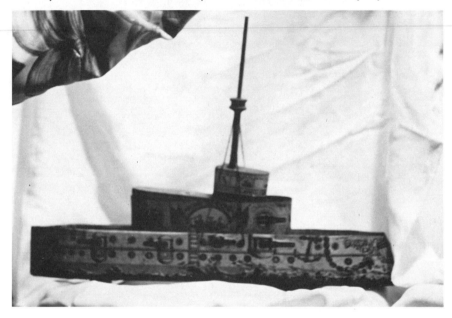

cap on its head. But later sailor dolls are more often seen, though the supply cannot be characterized as plentiful. In the first quarter of the twentieth century, sailor dolls were made in quantity and in a variety of materials—cloth, composition, rubber, celluloid, or a combination of such materials—and it is these dolls that are less expensive and more commonly found today. Often, however, they are in less than perfect condition and have lost some of their original clothing.

Most museums and restorations that feature old toys have boats of various materials on display, so it is relatively easy to get an idea of the types that were popular. At a recent antiques show I found two toy boats representing the *Puritan*, one made of iron and one of tin (Ills. 253 and 254). The *Puritan* was one of the fleet of the old Fall River Line that went between Boston and New York,

253. Tin toy—the *Puritan* of the Fall River Line. *Patricia and Sanford Smith Galleries, New York City*

254. This *Puritan* is made of iron. *Nina Hellman Antiques*

with stops at Newport and Fall River. An elderly man told me that he could remember seeing the Fall River Line boats from the flat where his family lived when he was a boy—and if a boat passed while they were at dinner, the meal was neglected as they watched the boat until it was out of sight. Many people can still remember traveling on the Fall River Line or having heard of it.

The ever-popular Noah's ark—a "nautical" toy in a category by itself—is sometimes found with its quaint people and animals intact. Some old ones can be definitely identified as American by their characteristic Pennsylvania Dutch workmanship.

There may have been nautical scenes and subjects in the class of collectibles known as paper toys, but little of this ephemera survives. Not long ago, one collector was lucky enough to discover a mint-condition early-1900s jigsaw puzzle of the *City of Worcester*, a side-wheeler with two stacks. McLoughlin Bros. of New York, the firm that made this puzzle, may well have produced others depicting contemporary ships, and doubtless other toy-and-game companies did too.

Personally, I know of no old games with nautical associations except for finely carved chess sets and Mah-Jongg sets brought here from the Orient or

255. The world's best publicized boat, Noah's ark, an excellent example of Pennsylvania Dutch workmanship as shown by the ornamentation of the roof and carving of the animals. *Orcutt Collection*

cribbage boards inlaid with ivory or mother-of-pearl. But interesting items do crop up. A friend of mine kept, for many years, a box containing some engraved elliptical pieces of mother-of-pearl that had belonged to her grandfather, the pilot of Queen Victoria's yacht. Although she had no idea what they were, they were nice to look at and feel—and so she resisted the temptation to donate them to a rummage sale or throw them away. Eventually, she saw disks just like them in a case in the Peabody Museum in Salem, on her first visit there. They were counters for a game, made by sailors. Perhaps the moral is: Never throw *anything* away until you have succeeded in identifying it.

MINIATURES

Miniatures might well be called the toys of adults. Not made for the wear and tear of children's play, they were wrought with care and precision for the delight of the grownup collector, to be displayed in cabinets or for decorative purposes.

256. Miniature ordnance is highly collectible. *San Francisco Maritime Museum*

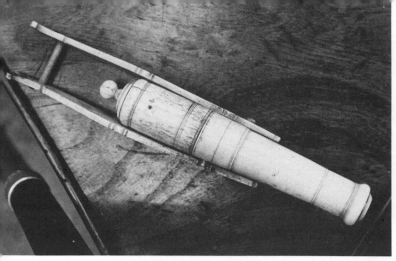

257. A scrimshaw cannon. Ordnance made by sailors from whalebone is most desirable, and seldom does a collector find a better example than this. *John Bihler & Henry Coger Antiques*

Many persons collect miniature ordnance. There are beautiful examples in the Mallory House of the Mystic Seaport Museum, mimicking the large cannons guarding the entrance. Ordnance replicas in a variety of small sizes were made early in our history, and they are still made, for these small weapons have real historical interest. Guns and cannons were used not only on warships, but on merchant ships as well. The danger of attack by pirates and privateers was a real one.

Quite different in the miniature line are the ships made by goldsmiths and jewelers. Many show great attention to detail, with correct rigging and billowing sails. Curiously, some extremely fine ship miniatures can be picked up at small cost. I bought an attractive model of a fishing schooner for twenty-five dollars. Yet, in the same year, jewelers were offering modern replicas—quite well done—for five hundred dollars.

258. Ships made of precious metal have found a ready market since the time of the early goldsmiths. Those that commemorate the achievements of a specific vessel are the most valuable. This silver miniature is approximately two inches high.

259. Some of the best-known miniature vessels are in the Crabtree Collection of The Mariners Museum in Newport News, Virginia. These models of every type of vessel were built piece by piece, from the keel up.

SHOES AND SEALING WAX

Ships on shoes and sealing wax—to take liberty with the Walrus—well, not really, but nearly. Not content with paintings and prints of ships, early craftsmen also used them to decorate various articles of furniture. Long before I became interested in the field, I saw a ladderback chair with a differently positioned ship painted on each of its back slats. The memory of lost opportunity still haunts me.

You may even pull a great find out of someone's ragbag—a piece of old chintz on which a boat is recorded. Chintzes became popular in the early nineteenth century because of the beautiful ones that the square-riggers brought to this country from India. Formerly, they had been imported from England, brought there by the great East India Trading Company. These chintzes inspired home manufacture. I have never seen a great travel print, but one was made and it was copied by the Index of American Design. It shows canal scenes and Mississippi riverboats of the early stern- and side-wheeler type.

Even today, collections are being made of material once passed by. Stamp collectors have gathered together interesting illustrations of the old shipping days made available by the United States Postal Service. Coins and medals with ships on them have a lively market. One of the earliest illustrations we have of a boat is on a medal.

260. A silver cup, decorated with a sailboat, is inscribed: "Won by the Weasel on the 17th of September, 1887. Owned by Thomas P. Calvert." Through such an heirloom, an ancestor's love of the sea came to light only when the tarnished old cup was polished.

261. A metal hatbox from the days of elegant queens of the sea, when plumes and flowers had to be protected from the salty breeze. *The John A. Reardon Collection*

262. Old clocks with a nautical past are rarely found. This one ticked for years in the lighthouse at Nauset, oblivious to the storms beyond the walls. *Mrs. Roy Davis*

8

PAINTINGS FOR PROFIT
AND PLEASURE

POSSIBLY THE MOST SOUGHT AFTER of all nautical antiques are paintings and prints of the vessels of yesteryear. Nothing proclaims more quietly and authoritatively "We are collectors of nauticals" than the likeness of a square-rigger in full sail, or if you're a small-boat enthusiast, a yacht rounding the southwest buoy. What conversation pieces they prove to be! A desire for more knowledge about your print or painting can start you on a new path of exploration. It never winds in quite the same direction for any collector.

The chapters here on paintings and prints with sea as subject are the pointer in your hand. Together with the illustrations, they will give you a "feel" for one of the most expansive pursuits in the nautical field. It is a field for the speculator too, and alas, there's a little bit of that in any collector. Buy what you like if you can. Recently, I refrained—and lost. In a little antiques shop I saw an interesting painting in blue monochrome of a fishing schooner. "Fifteen dollars," said the dealer. "It's rather good, don't you think?" But I was not in a buying mood.

Six weeks later, on the other side of the continent, in the prestigious San Francisco Maritime Museum, I found a painting by the same hand. The blue monochrome was both unforgettable and compelling. But the museum was closing; I never did learn the name of the painter. Back home, I phoned the dealer in the little shop—the painting was gone.

Perhaps you have never thought of buying a work of art. A painting or print worthy of such a classification, you say, is beyond your means or your knowledge. The way to banish this self-imposed blockade to collecting is to visit a marine museum and look at the variety of interpretations of the nautical scene, both for quality and subject matter.

"There are some painters who transform the sun into a yellow spot, but there are others who, thanks to their art and intelligence, transform the yellow spot into the sun," Pablo Picasso once said. Just so, some small drawing or painting that strikes your fancy can bring you the full majesty of the sea, the intimacy of its wave crests, the fierceness of its power.

It is the way the painting affects *you* that makes it important. Nor is this a novel way to judge a piece of art. The director of the Boston Museum of Fine Arts said, in an interview, that he *knows* a piece of sculpture or painting is *good* only when it has been in the museum for some time, when he has looked at it, studied it under different lights, in different surroundings. Such a test is one that the novice in collecting nautical antiques can apply to what he buys, especially

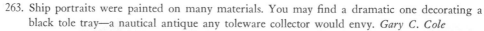

263. Ship portraits were painted on many materials. You may find a dramatic one decorating a black tole tray—a nautical antique any toleware collector would envy. *Gary C. Cole*

264. *Along the River* (a scene near Harpers Ferry) is noteworthy because, although it was done in 1840, it is charcoal on sandpaper, a technique a hundred years ahead of its time. River scenes often include other interesting details besides the watercraft. Note the crude bridge. *Collection of Hirschl and Adler Galleries, New York*

if he looks not only at his new purchase, but continues to look and look at other nautical paintings and prints wherever he can find them. When Paul J. Sachs was professor of fine arts at Harvard, he used to point out to his students, "The eye is best trained through an intimate knowledge of the finest of the genre."

As you work to become a connoisseur, two qualities are necessary—discrimination and understanding. Time and again they seem to come slowly, but there are guideposts to help. A collector is both helped and deceived, however, by an innate love of the sea. Usually it helps. Whether a painting or print is realistic or abstract, traditional or experimental, your instinct is the best guide to quality or "phoniness" if you know the sea.

Even in the 1870s, marine painters were experimenting with different mediums to achieve the effects they wanted. Cardboard was pasted onto canvas very much like a modern collage; paintings were made on sandpaper to create the feeling of the sea.

By living with a painting or print you will soon know whether you have discovered great art in some out-of-the-way place, or whether it is just a blue and white spot on the wall. If the latter is the case, you can probably sell your "mistake." Often you will be surprised at your good investing sense. Some years ago I bought a pair of pictures in a small antiques shop for what seemed to me a respectable sum—four hundred dollars. The pictures showed two Esquimaux, with plains and sea in the background. They were signed, but I paid little attention to the signature. For a long time they hung on our walls, unnoticed by visitors and the family alike. But as I looked at them in a vague sort of way one day, the name of the artist dawned in all its significance. It was important—Cornelius Krieghoff, one of the great early Canadian painters.

In the end, the signature paid off. I sold the two paintings to a dealer for twelve hundred dollars, which seemed a fortune to me at the time, but apparently it was a cheap price. The dealer sold them to another dealer, that dealer to still another. Who knows what they were really worth, or where they are now?

This is not an unusual story in the field of marine art. A man who has been specializing in such discoveries for years tells me that he always doubles his money in selling a painting, sometimes triples it, and often indeed does much better.

Among the great interpreters of the sea is Winslow Homer. Stand before one of his paintings to learn how one man's vision can be translated onto canvas with such skill and feeling that it matches your own. In the same little antiques shop of the Krieghoff purchase, we once bought a painting that reminded us of Homer—the rendering of the waves, for instance, and the typical Winslow Homer boys. The dealer knew no more about it than that she had bought it in a sale of household goods.

While other paintings came and went in our home, the "almost Homer" continued to delight us. Then one evening we were photographing some plants with an array of fluorescent and incandescent lamps. I happened to look up at the painting. There, on the right-hand corner, brought out by the fall of light, was what appeared to be the signature Winslow Homer. Although we have not had the signature verified, we nonetheless think of the painting as "our Homer."

Signatures are important, and learning to recognize, decipher, and ferret them out is a career in itself. I have aimed high in my own particular quest for the undiscovered work of one painter, Thomas Thompson. The New York harbor was his principal interest, and he painted it in a grand panorama of sloops and square-riggers. There is tremendous beauty of color in his massive work in the collection of the Metropolitan Museum of Art.*

Thompson was said to be a prolific painter. I thought, of course, some of his works must be round about, but I've come to believe what the art critics

---

* *A Catalog of the Metropolitan Museum of Art* by Albert Ten Eyck Gardner and Stuart B. Field. Illustrated. Page 128.

265. Each nautical collector likes to include in his or her collection a painting that shows the majesty of the sea. William Richards ranks high as a nineteenth-century painter of seascapes. As in this canvas, he shows the power of the ocean yet suggests its tragedy with floating jetsam of some lost ship in the foreground. *Lake View Galleries*

say, that "very few of his works have survived." Still, the thought lingers that some did survive and their whereabouts are unknown.

You can be encouraged by the knowledge that we have had many great American painters of sea and ships. Though you may not find masterpieces, there are excellent seascapes for sale at small sums and large. It is the enthusiasm that the painter conveys in his watercolor or oil that touches the heart in this kinship of sea lovers. Even one such painting, or one good print hanging on your wall, makes you a collector of nautical antiques.

"How can I know whether or not I am buying trash?" The answer is ever the same: Whether you know much, or only a little, success lies in buying what you like. In the fine arts, love can take you a long way. The heart often grasps what the mind has not reached.

No one insists that most of the old-time maritime painters were giants among artists. Some were, but many of them well conveyed the appeal of the sea and the hard grueling life of a seaman. There are other reasons for finding and owning nautical paintings. For one thing, they tell the story of our nation. Those painted in America before the Revolution are rare indeed. Painting historic naval events came into its own with the War of 1812, which was largely a naval

266. An especially inspired example of a painting of the War of 1812, so many of which were based on Thomas Birch's concept of the conflict. A rare painting. *Newport Historical Society*

267. A representation of the capture of the U.S. Corvette *Wasp* on October 18, 1812. The original watercolor is in the United States Naval Museum. Such imaginative depictions of 1812 battle scenes have remained popular.

268. The surrender of the British frigate *Macedonian* to the frigate *United States,* October 25, 1812. Another picture in the series of battle scenes in the United States Naval Museum at Annapolis.

war. Paintings and prints could scarcely be finished fast enough to tell an eager nation just what was happening. Among those who painted the triumphs achieved by our ships with their guns were Thomas Birch, Michele Corné, Thomas Sully, Thomas Chambers, J. J. Bartlett, and many others less generally known. Because prints were made of these artists' works, their names were circulated throughout the states. Two other artists, George Thresher and George Roupes, who earlier were classified as "primitive painters" because they had not had formal artistic training, are eagerly sought today, now that folk art has found its place. They too painted naval encounters.

The victory of the *Constitution* over the *Guerrière* warmed the heart of every American. Thomas Birch, one of the excellent early painters from Philadelphia, immortalized this and other victories of the War of 1812. Many artists followed his interpretations, and countless prints were made from his paintings. They continued to be made even into the 1850s. Representations of the victory of the *Constitution* are found also on porcelain, pottery, glass, and scrimshaw.

In the first fifty years of the nineteenth century, the years when a new nation was forming and growing, painting, prints, and drawings were the only means of delineating the events of the day. They comprise a field that always beckons to collectors.

Paintings of the War of 1812 were scarcely done "on the spot." They were accurate enough, however, to satisfy the waiting public when engravers made prints of them. Prior to that time, most of the early paintings and prints of American defeats and victories had borne the signatures of English artists. There are relatively few even of these.

269. Oil painting on canvas of the American packet ship *Samoset,* built by Fernald & Petti-
grew of Portsmouth, New Hampshire, painted around 1850 by Samuel Walters, R. A.
(1811–1882). Paintings of ships were probably the earliest nautical antiques to be collected.
You will find them on the walls of all museums. Some are hard to resist, whatever your
specialty may be. *Mystic Seaport photograph, Mystic, Connecticut*

SHIP PORTRAITURE

To the captain of a ship, the desire for a portrait of her was as great as a
mother's desire for one of her child. Whenever he had a new commission, he
ordered the ship's portrait painted. Thus it is not uncommon to find portraits of
the same ship identified with different captains' names.

Because of the fine record they give us of ships of the past, ship portraits
have both interest and value. They also tell us something of the ports of the
world, for it was a popular custom to have a ship's portrait made in a foreign
port. In Holland, in France, in Spain, in Italy, in far-off China and Japan,
artists stood waiting for commissions to paint the picture of any ship that
arrived in port, for painting ship portraits was a cosmopolitan art. The captains
of many countries felt there were no better souvenirs to take home than portraits of their ships done in foreign ports.

Ships, like people sitting for portraits, were posed in certain conventional

270. If you find a painting, carefully done in every detail, of a ship with all sails set for the wind—staid and proper, devoid of all action—you have an American ship portrait of the nineteenth century. Usually they are beautifully framed. This one of a schooner is an excellent example—how a master wanted his ship to look. *Cornelia Black, Westchester Commission Mart Antiques*

ways in eighteenth- and nineteenth-century works of art. In many of the paintings, the ship is shown in two views—first broadside, and a second time coming about. Some nineteenth-century portraits show three aspects—broadside, coming about, and as a small ship far in the background. In others, the ship that is coming about is omitted, and only the small replica far in the back-

271. The tragedy of shipwreck is simply told in this painting by Edward Moran of the survivors in *Shipwreck off Long Island*. *Lake View Galleries*

272. Sometimes a portrait nearly comes alive, as does this one of the *Jeannie R. DuBois*. *The Mariners Museum, Newport News, Virginia*

ground is shown as a secondary feature. Of course, innumerable ship portraits were made only broadside—a square-rigger in full sail will cover the entire canvas. Because these portraits were usually accurate representations, they are treasured both by museums and by individuals for their home or office (Ill. 270).

The oldest known American ship portrait is preserved in the Peabody Museum in Salem. It is *The Letter of Marque Ship "Bethel" of Boston, 14 guns.* The *Bethel* was launched at Portsmouth, New Hampshire, in 1748. It qualifies in the nomenclature of "ship portraiture" because the ship is shown in two views. In the first position it is broadside; then it is shown slightly to the side and coming about. Although there is no question that innumerable single views of ships were *portraits*, the term is more accurately applied to those paintings that show more than one view of the same ship.

One of the well-known painters of American ships in foreign ports was

273. Few were the sights that could equal the beauty of a ship under many sails. She captured the hearts of Americans, as she sailed to port after port around the world. This impressive portrait is by an unknown artist.

Antoine Roux (1765–1835). He made portraits of ships that stopped at Marseilles from all over the world, but his chief customers were Americans. His two sons worked with him, and together they turned out a tremendous amount of work. Roux particularly pleased his clientele because of the technical sense he had of the vessels he was painting. With this technical sense he combined an artistic rendering of the background—the sea and the sky. His portraits of ships are considered excellent art.

Two of the artists who made ship portraits in America long after the camera knocked many of their brethren out of the field were Antonio Jacobsen (Ill. 277), who so picturesquely covered New York harbor on horseback, and John Henry Mohrmas, who was born in San Francisco, went abroad, and came back to continue making ship portraits. Jacobsen, who came rather late into painting steamships, would no doubt have been astonished could he have foreseen that in

274. Behind the beauty of the square-rigger, a steamship glides almost unnoticed, a prophetic force, in a painting by L. A. *Lake View Galleries*

The Situation of the Dellaware Steamers after She was first struck in the White Squall, being about Six...

275. The U.S.S. *Dellaware* is here pictured on her homeward journey, fifteen minutes after being hit by a squall. This is one of a pair of paintings by J. G. Evans. The name of the ship is spelled differently on the two pictures. *Newport Historical Society*

slightly less than a hundred years, his pictures of ships and the sea would be selling in New York shops for $2,500 and more. He was a prolific painter. As business boomed, he rented a horse to ride from one end of New York harbor to the other, to greet and paint new ships coming into port. Rare was the captain who did not want his ship portrayed by this well-known and talented artist. When business was slow, Jacobsen anticipated modern methods—he painted backdrops of sea and waves, sky and clouds, against which he could later paint in the actual ship. Practically all his work is signed, but the very sameness of his backgrounds is a good identifying feature of a Jacobsen.

Lest you think that so expensive a treasure is not for you, do not forget the strange largesse that is often a part of antique hunting. One of the research associates from a museum was on Cape Cod doing some work when he chanced on a framed Jacobsen steamship painting in a garbage can. Honorably, he rescued it and called upon the owner of the garbage pail—and the priceless painting—to apprise him of the picture's value.

276. *Homeward Bound*, by C. Drew, 1878. Minot's Ledge and Boston Lights are in the distance. *Hilbert Brothers Collection*

277. In this painting of a steamship by Antonio Jacobsen the insignia on the smokestack can be clearly seen. It is far more prominent than the small house flag. The asking price for Jacobsen paintings today is $2,000 and up. *Patricia and Sanford Smith Galleries, New York City*

"Take it along," the owner said. "I just don't like that painting."

Portraits of ship captains are highly collectible too, as are harbor scenes and paintings of lighthouses. Traditionally, portraits of sea captains have a ship of some sort, commonly the captain's own vessel, in the background, or the man himself may hold a nautical instrument in his hands. Portraits of this kind are often cherished as family heirlooms, and so do not come on the market very frequently (Ills. 280 and 281).

278. *Schooners in the Harbor* by Louis Feuchter, 1882, has the photographic detail of much of the marine art of the period. *The Mariners Museum, Newport News, Virginia*

279. Paintings of lighthouses have been in great demand throughout the nineteenth and twentieth centuries. Some of the best American artists painted them. This pastel of the Portland Light has the kind of quality collectors appreciate.

280. Paintings of ship captains have been in demand from the seventeenth century to the present. Though the earlier examples are hard to find, collectors appreciate the aura surrounding those from the nineteenth century. This portrait shows a captain with his spyglass under his arm and his ship in the background, traditional features in a portrait of a sea captain. *Allan L. Daniel*

281. Portrait of Sherburne Sears (1806–1888) is in the elegant tradition, with the sea as background and a ship in the distance. It was painted in 1835 by Jean Pierre Feulard when Sears's ship was in Le Havre. *John Bihler & Henry Coger Antiques*

9

AMERICAN PRINTS FOR NAUTICAL COLLECTORS

PRINTS HAVE A ROYAL LINEAGE stretching far back in time, but for all practical purposes the ninth-century woodcuts of China stand as the illustrious beginning. It was several centuries before the method of making these prints reached Europe. Then the art flowered in the works of Albrecht Dürer and Hans Holbein.

By the time the colonists settled in America, the making of woodcuts had become familiar, particularly for illustrating books. As early as 1677, a book printed by John Foster of Boston carried as frontispiece a woodcut map of New England. Only in England at that time were woodcuts printed separately as "pictures." For today's collector of prints, seventeenth-century American examples are practically nonexistent.

The famous woodcut map of New England by Foster appeared in William Hubbard's book, *A Narrative of the Troubles with the Indians in New England.* It covers a large portion of New England, from Maine to the Connecticut River, inland and along the coastline, including Boston Harbor, Cape Cod, and Long Island Sound to a short way beyond the mouth of the Connecticut River.

Old maps are the love not only of geographers and historians but of nautical collectors as well. You will find them on the walls of all marine museums, and as the prize possessions of many collectors. All are examples of early en-

282. *The Bay and River of Delaware* is typical of the type of map by which masters sailed in the nineteenth century. This map appeared in an old book. *Orcutt Collection*

graving, yet surprisingly few have survived. There are only a few known copies of Foster's original map of New England. One is in the John Carter Brown Library in Providence. The map is known as the "White Hills" map because of its depiction of the White Hills, looking like two round mounds of earth, at the side of the work. Had not an English version of Foster's map referred to the hills as the "Wine Hills," they might not have been noticed, but the misprint is a means of distinguishing the two versions. Several early vessels are also shown in Foster's map. The illuminating of most early maps is somewhat crude but delightful, adding to the charm.

Woodcuts were used for other forms of engraving. Foster is credited with the first woodcut to be made in America, a signed portrait of the clergyman and writer Richard Mather. He also engraved the Massachusetts Colonial currency, and was known for his work on coats of arms.

Many other woodcuts are known, but they are anonymous. They were used as billheads, trade cards, and book illustrations. Even Benjamin Franklin is credited with making woodcuts in his printing shop.

In making a woodcut, the design is drawn on the plank side of a piece of wood. To make this stand out, the surrounding areas are cut away. When complete, the picture, lettering, or map stands out in relief, as type does in the familiar printing process. Ink is applied, a paper is laid on the block, and by means of pressure or rubbing the design is transferred to the paper. It is much like the steps you take in making a Christmas card from a linoleum block. Nevertheless, this homely method was man's first achievement in multiple printing. That very fact makes any nautical woodcut a meaningful addition to a collection.

Line engraving on copper provided a second means of multiple printing. The results obtained are more precise than those from woodcutting, and line engraving immediately became prized as a means for making maps and illustrations. In the Middle Ages, jewelers working with metals engraved lines and filled them with gold. Copper line engraving is an adaptation of this idea. The engraved lines are filled with ink instead of gold.

In making a line engraving, the artist or map maker plows the lines of his design into a burnished copper plate with a tool called a burin. The incisions are filled with ink, the surface of the plate is wiped clean, a paper is put over it, and the whole is put into a press, the design being transferred to the paper by pressure. The black lines of the print stand up on the paper—you can actually feel them by running your finger over them. If the print has been framed behind glass, you can still distinguish these raised lines with a good magnifying glass.

Althea Helster, in charge of prints at the Buffalo and Erie County Historical Society, tells the story of the first line engraving to be produced in the pioneer city of Buffalo, New York. Sheldon Bell was the craftsman. The year was about 1825. The scene was Buffalo Harbor (Ill. 283). Having studied the technique of line engraving from the sources then available, Bell set out on his own to prepare and engrave a plate. He carried it up the stairs to the shop of Buffalo's first printer. Together, they worked to make the print, only to be disappointed in the result. The fault turned out to be with the ink. With time and effort, the right ink was obtained, the plate run through the printer's press, and the charming print reproduced here was the result.

283. View of Buffalo Harbor in 1825, by Sheldon Bell, the first engraving to be made in the city of Buffalo. A copper line engraving, it well illustrates the technique. *Buffalo and Erie County Historical Society*

VIEW OF BUFFALO HARBOR.

Ten years or so later, in 1833 or 1836, William Bennett, whose work is discussed later in this chapter, made a beautiful aquatint of the Buffalo harbor scene (see Ill. 289).

The Columbia River Maritime Museum in Astoria, Oregon, exhibits an original copperplate from which charts of the mouth of the Columbia River were struck. It was engraved in 1851 by McCuller and Bartlett of the newly formed United States Survey Office. The dazzling copper with its many reflections does not obscure the lines of the river's course, and in one glance a person can vividly see the full scope of a copperplate line engraving. I tried to take a picture of this copperplate so that others might share with me both its beauty and its information, but the sparkling reflections would let me have none of it. However, watch your chance. If the artist is skilled, both the engraved plate and the engraving made from it are beautiful.

As one can see if he scans early newspapers, interest in engravings ran high in the Colonies. In the New York *Packet* of June 1, 1797, appeared an announcement of Peter Maverick; "the subscriber, ever willing to serve the public," respectfully informed them that he carried on "engraving, seal sinking, and copper plate printing at No. 3 Crown Street." And the *Boston Register,* July 10 1794, published this advertisement:

> Copper plates – – – To the Publisher and Printer of Periodical Works to be sold very cheap, a great variety of copper plates, engraved by the best artists and in good condition, suitable to any periodical publication. These plates 124 in number originally cost engravers upwards of one thousand pounds sterling, and may now be had at a very reduced price.

The Revolutionary War and the forming of a new nation brought a dramatic change in printmaking in America. New engraving methods were learned from Europe, and capable artists and engravers undertook the work. Public interest was so great that the first half of the nineteenth century has been called The Golden Age of Engraving in America.

As if to say farewell to the old and welcome to the new, William and Thomas Birch, father and son, drew, engraved, and published a set of twenty-eight line engravings, *The City of Philadelphia as it appears in 1800.* This project introduced the name of Birch, which was to play such an important part in

284. This quiet harbor view of Fort Niagara on the Niagara River belies the fact that it was the scene of some of the hottest battles in the War of 1812. *Ballou's Pictorial Drawing-Room Companion, 1850*

285. An engraving of Fort Ontario on New York's Oswego River depicts both small sailing craft and larger boats combining steam and sail. At the time of the War of 1812, forts were built on many American rivers that were close to the border. Both this and the preceding print were signed by Kilburn. *Ballou's Pictorial Drawing-Room Companion, 1850*

the painting and engraving field of the nineteenth century. These engravings were reissued by Birch and, in 1841, by DeSilver. Many of them are of interest to marine scene enthusiasts and are well worth seeking, but they are not cheap.

In spite of the popularity of the woodcut and the line engraving, three other art forms were to capture the American fancy and provide the pictorial records of nineteenth-century events and manners sought by collectors today. The aquatint, the lithograph, and the wood-engraving processes, which originated in Europe, flowered in a profusion of illustrations and prints that delight and inform present-day collectors and historians as they did the original viewers.

A nautical print can be many things—a nostalgic memory of bygone years, a Currier and Ives lithograph of *The Golden Age of Sail*, a delicately tinted wood engraving of a very small schooner and a mighty square-rigger, a framed aquatint of *A Shoal of Sperm Whales off the Island of Harvaii*—a real find among nineteenth-century prints, though you might not expect it with Hawaii spelled wrong.

286. The choppy waters of Lake Michigan dominate this engraved view of the Chicago skyline of yesteryear. *Ballou's Pictorial Drawing-Room Companion, 1850*

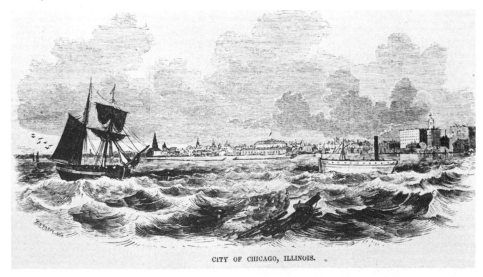

CITY OF CHICAGO, ILLINOIS.

VIEW OF VICKSBURG, MISSISSIPPI.

287. Nineteenth-century engravings of river ports along the Mississippi generally feature the dramatic steamboats with their plumes of black, black smoke. *Gleason's Pictorial Drawing-Room Companion, 1850*

288. Wood engraving of Baltimore harbor in the days of sail. *Gleason's Pictorial Drawing-Room Companion, 1850*

VIEW OF THE CITY OF BALTIMORE

AQUATINTS

The development of the aquatint by Jean Baptiste Le Prince (1733–1781) came about in a manner worthy of a Hollywood film scenario. On a trip to Russia, the ship in which Le Prince was a passenger was captured by pirates. He was transferred to their ship, clutching his favorite possessions—his engraving tools, metal, paper, and his violin. While on the pirate ship, Le Prince so charmed his captors with his violin playing that he was allowed to continue to work on his etchings. The conditions were scarcely those of a studio. When he pulled a proof, dust on the etching plate produced the effect of a network of etched lines. It looked amazingly like a drawing. Le Prince must have exclaimed to himself: "This is a masterpiece!" What a moment of triumph it must have been: alone, a prisoner on a pirate ship, and to pull a proof that was one of the most beautiful etchings he had produced.

The problem was to do it again. Le Prince knew that the effect had come from the dust that had settled on the plate, but how does one control dust? He spent his time figuring ways to create miniature dust storms. It was a simple contrivance that he devised—a small box with a handle that made the dust fly. On a slightly heated resined plate, the dust settled in specks and globules. By just this means, the aquatint was born. By the time Le Prince was released in France, he had perfected the process. His invention was well received and, in storybook fashion, he was able to retire to a beautiful villa, there to live as a respected and honored master.

Aquatints immediately became popular in France, England, and Germany. It was Edward Savage, painter and engraver (1761–1817), who brought the process to America. Inspired by the unusual results obtained in prints made with Le Prince's process, Savage decided to learn how it was done, even though this involved his going to Europe to study. He studied in both London and Italy from 1791 to 1794. His popular aquatint *Action Between the "Constellation" and "L'Insurgent"* was published in 1799. Savage became an apostle of the aquatint process—he made aquatints himself, taught others, answered questions, and in general was effective in establishing the new process here.

William James Bennett* (1787–1844), an English artist who came to America in 1816, was both a painter and an engraver of aquatints. His series of views of American cities are regarded by many as the finest colored aquatints in this field. The one shown here, from the collection of the Buffalo and Erie County Historical Society, is an outstanding example: *Buffalo from Lake Erie,* 1833. He is also known for *Street Views in the City of New York,* published by H. J. Megary, New York, in 1834; two views of the Great Fire in New York in December, 1835, after N. W. Calyo; and *The Seasons,* after George Harvey, 1844.

Because so many aquatints were city scenes, often including views of harbors and their teeming lives, these prints offer many possibilities to collectors of nautical antiques. Relatively few were made after 1850, a fact that emphasizes their historical value.

Aquatints printed in black and white almost resemble India ink drawings.

---

* "Engravings" by Elizabeth R. Roth in *Concise Encyclopedia of American Antiques,* vol. 2 (New York: Hawthorn Books, Inc.), p. 355.

289. An aquatint of Buffalo Harbor made by William Bennett around 1836. It is one of a series of harbor prints made by Bennett, all of which he printed and hand colored. He is known for his colored aquatints, which are considered the finest in the field. *Buffalo and Erie County Historical Society*

One that I saw of a fire in New York, with beautiful black outlines and water-color-tinted flames, still haunts me. In addition to black and white, aquatints were also printed in two colors, earth and sky tints, the others being supplied by hand. A few were made with more than two color plates, but the general custom was to paint in the rest of the colors by hand.

An aquatint may at first seem more difficult to identify than other engravings, but careful inspection will eliminate any confusion. Again, you look at the engraved lines. An aquatint has a velvety-appearing surface, caused in part by the texture of the lines. The stylus used is different from that used in cutting other engravings. The lines are thin, gracefully drawn out, almost feathery. But the real identification is in the breakage of these lines; there—though almost imperceptible—are dots, granules, bits: the effect Le Prince achieved with his "dust storms."

Aquatints are among the most beautiful of engravings. Once you have seen one, you may not be satisfied until you have one of your own. It is almost as if an aura of romance lingers from the time that Le Prince, the pirates' captive, made his strange discovery.

LITHOGRAPHS

The lithograph could well be called the American print. From 1819, when the first lithograph was made in the United States by Bass Otis, until nearly the end of the century, when other art forms took over, it was the darling of the

American people—admired, bought, framed, hung everywhere from parlors to outhouses, preserved, enjoyed, and, as the taste changed, thrown away. One hundred and fifty years later it is a prize sought by collectors as the best known of the antique prints made in America in the nineteenth century.

Interest in all nineteenth-century lithographs is high, but those made by Currier and Ives are particularly valued (Ills. 290 and 291). N. Currier founded the firm in New York in 1834. In 1857, he took James Ives into partnership, and from that time the firm's prints were known as Currier and Ives. Harry T. Peters,* whose books on the subject did so much to create interest in these literal records of their time, considered them social documents describing in pictorial detail an age that is past. This characteristic of Currier and Ives prints has made them particularly appealing to twentieth-century collectors, and so they are high-priced today.

Originally, because they were so cheap, the prints were not reproduced. The small prints were sold to hawkers, wholesale, for six cents apiece. In later years, when the prints were reproduced, the names of the printing firms making the reproductions were usually printed underneath. They have been reproducd in their original colors and sizes, in large books, with no text printed on the back of the pictures so that they can be cut out for framing.

In 1936, The Travelers Insurance Company began its practice of reproducing important Currier and Ives prints on its annual calendars. So colorful and accurate are these scenes that, according to an antiques dealer, "old" prints from the calendars can readily be sold. Of course, there is a vast difference in price between collectibles of this later variety and authentic Currier and Ives prints.

Collectors of Currier and Ives nautical prints like the careful detail of the rigging and of the sails of each vessel—from the yacht *America* to the clippers with their graceful bows and raked masts reaching upward for more driving power. Nautical lithographs are sometimes more dramatic than literal, however, as Peter C. Welsh pointed out in the magazine *Antiques* (September, 1961): "Unlike the photograph, the lithograph is always of questionable veracity, and the line that separates the real from the imagined is frequently obscured. For instance, warfare to the lithographer's eye became a pageant stripped of grimness." This softened reality perhaps accounts for the popularity of prints of naval warfare—the destruction of vessels and lives, the sinkings, the explosions, all tempered by art.

Then, too, the lithograph brought the news of the day in straight yellow-journalism fashion. Everyone wanted to see what was happening, as soon as possible, and like today's television producers, the lithographers did their best to accommodate.

* Harry T. Peters, *Currier & Ives, Printmakers to the American People* (Garden City, New York: Doubleday, 1929).

Some of America's best artists were employed to make the drawings and paintings that were transferred to the lithographer's stone, usually by the artist himself, sometimes by a skilled employee of the firm. By the mid-fifties, lithographs were at the height of their popularity. Artists such as Daniel MacFarland and James Buttersworth were sent to cover disasters, ship launchings, vessels that made astonishing round-trip records to the Orient, to San Francisco, to Liverpool. Thus the prints are often eyewitness reports of the world of yesterday. These pictorial reporters were merely trying to fill the news needs of their countrymen. Unwittingly, they were making not only collectors' items but important historical documents.

The great majority of lithographs were printed in black and white and colored by hand. At Currier and Ives, a group of twelve girls, under the justly

290. A lithograph was drawn on stone with a specially prepared crayon. The fact that the drawing was done with a crayon gives a lithograph its special identification. It does not have the fineness of line of an engraving. If you look carefully at the Currier and Ives print of the famous race between the *Natchez* and the *Robert E. Lee,* you will see that the lines are sharp, but minute detail is lacking. Another aid in identification is the legend beneath the print. Usually there is the title, often (but not always) followed by the firm's name and the address. *Orcutt Collection*

famous Fanny Palmer, sat around a table, each ready to put on one color. Light-fast colors were imported from Austria, with the result that the colors of Currier and Ives prints are brighter and tend to stand up better than those of other makers. In these brightly colored prints, the lines stand out, tenuous yet sharp. Study a Currier and Ives print when you next visit a marine museum. It will not be long before you will be able to recognize a lithograph. Many times you will also know whether or not it was made by the great Currier and Ives firm.

Alfred R. Davison of East Aurora, New York, who has spent years in the study of Currier and Ives prints, assures beginners that it is not too late to find some excellent prints at affordable prices. In the last fifty years, he has handled more than eight thousand prints, and he knows well the guidelines for wise choices.

"Nautical collectors are in a good field," Mr. Davison says. "Currier and Ives clippers rank with the railroads as best-selling prints. Clipper ships are hard to find, and expensive, but steamship prints can be bought for fifty to seventy-five dollars. Since clipper ships are selling at high prices, this field may offer a good subject for investment.

"A number of things influence price. Death scenes, religious pictures, and foreign scenes should be avoided. In most cases a beginner cannot go wrong in buying the best he can afford. He is reasonably sure of making a profit later.

"Sizes of Currier and Ives prints differ slightly. Three were standard: the small folio, with the colored section approximately 8 by 12 inches; the medium-sized folio, about 11 by 15 inches; and the large folio, 20 by 28 inches or some-times 20 by 30 inches. Large folio prints are the most expensive. As a compari-son, in the same week that I sold a large folio print of the *Midnight Race on the Mississippi* for $750, I sold a small folio of the same print for $50.

"Uncut margins are preferable. Generally the margins reached from 3 to 3½ inches beyond the picture proper. Picture framers of the period wanted to use 10- by 14-inch frames, and consequently the prints were often cut to size. Value has bowed to the custom, and contrary to common belief, cut margins do not detract much from value if a print is in good condition, has at least an inch of margin all around, and the inscription beneath it.

"The company copyrighted prints that they thought would sell well. It worked out that about 50 percent of their prints were copyrighted. All copy-rights have run out, and the prints can be copied, but it is possible to distinguish a copy from an original. Among the details to look for are the small dots that make up the picture. Both originals and copies are composed of dots, but in the originals the dots are irregular and smaller than those in the reproductions, which are all even, the same size.

"The color of the paper also affords a clue. In originals the paper is white and rather thick; in reproductions it tends to be lighter and cream in tone. Value is lessened in torn or otherwise damaged prints. Stains, which often can be removed, are less significant.

291. Currier and Ives print of the *Swallow* disaster, a best-selling print in its day. *Nina Hellman Antiques*

"Buyers should also consider the dates of Currier and Ives prints. The earliest were by N. Currier, from 1835 to 1857, when Ives joined the firm. In 1885, the Currier sons took over the business, and the quality of the prints deteriorated. Color printing methods of the day supplanted the former hand coloring. About this time, the sons issued the Negro comics that are in demand today. By 1907, the firm was through, and other prints held the center stage.

"The magic of the Currier and Ives name makes a print sell better than equally good prints by competitors, which, however, should not be rejected. All are interesting illustrations of other times, other ways."

One finds bargains in lithographs, particularly in those made by other companies of the period. Small plants sprang up early in all the major cities. Unfortunately for nautical collectors, they did not make many prints of ships or the sea, though there are some charming ones of rivers, ferryboats, and smaller craft. E. B. and E. C. Kellogg of Hartford, New York, and Buffalo, founded in 1833, was the second largest producer of lithographs. But this is not the company that is remembered as next in popular esteem. That honor goes to the Endicott Company. Nautical collectors, in particular, prize the Endicott lithographs, for the firm made more than a thousand different nautical prints. The Curriers were acclaimed for their portrayal of the beautiful clippers; the Endicotts, for their rendering of the steamship.

The first great Currier success—this was before Ives was taken into the firm —was the print *Awful Conflagration of the Steam Boat "Lexington" in Long*

Island Sound on Monday Eve'g Jan. 13th, 1840, by which melancholy Occur-rance over 100 persons perished. Quite a title! The presses turned out the print night and day. Like a newspaper, it was hawked in the streets of New York. N. Currier "became a national institution." We do not know how many prints were made, but it was doubtless the largest edition of any print up to that time.

Try, however, to find one of these prints today. Yet the unexpected does happen. Currier's *Burning of the Henry Clay Near Yonkers, on July 28, 1852, a disaster in which many were lost, including Stephen Allen, a former mayor of New York* was found by an eastern New York dealer, and a few months later the same dealer found another identical print.

My brother-in-law, helping a friend dispose of some things from her attic,

292. Two lithographs of Newport, Rhode Island, by J. P. Newall, an outstanding but less well-known lithographer of marine scenes. *Newport Historical Society*

pried up a loose floorboard and there found a folio print of *The Midnight Race on the Mississippi,* which pictures the race between the *Natchez* and the *Eclipse.* The feeling of suspense that dominated the races of the side-wheelers from New Orleans to Saint Louis is captured. The black vessels, the orange glow from the engines, the banners of smoke from the stacks, all silhouetted against silvery moonlight breaking through the clouds, epitomize the drama and color of the early days on the Mississippi. The finders sold the print for a mere thirty-five dollars and felt that they had done very well. As the dealer said, "It's a good print, but you know there's not much color in it."

It should be noted that among known Currier and Ives prints there are more than four hundred on marine subjects—steamships, sailing ships, yachts, the United States Navy, whaling. Others related to the Revolutionary, Mexican, and Civil wars might also tie in at points with a nautical collection. Specific information may be found in *Currier and Ives Prints—An Illustrated Check List,* by Frederic A. Conningham (updated by Colin Simkin).*

The pioneer lithographer in the United States was W. S. Pendleton, who, after studying the process in England and France, opened the first lithographic printing shop in partnership with his brother. His first print was of one of Robert Fulton's steamships, the *Chancellor Livingston.* Fulton's first successful steamship, the *Clermont,* had steamed up the Hudson to Albany on August 11, 1807, the voyage taking thirty-two hours, as already mentioned. The *Chancellor Livingston,* one of nine later ships whose building was supervised by Fulton, was the first to have a regular course on Long Island Sound, from New York to Providence. It was a source of pride to New Englanders, and the Pendleton print, if found by a collector, would be a find indeed.

The chromolithograph, which was popular in the 1860s, was printed in at least two different colors, sometimes more, but usually brown and blue, or green and blue. The method required drawing on two or more stones and careful registering of the prints. Hand-coloring was sometimes applied as well.

The special lithographic process gave very special results. To me this was particularly apparent in a large loan exhibit of Currier and Ives prints, from western New York collectors, held at the Kenan Center in Lockport in 1973. The show brought together varied and important prints, including a large number of nauticals: yachts that won the America's Cup Race with the insignia of the New York Yacht Club in the legend beneath the print; a scene of the great *Swallow* disaster; and many clippers and square-riggers.

A name for lovers of lithographs to remember is that of Aloys Senefelder (1771–1834), who is generally conceded to be the inventor of lithography. A Bohemian, born in Prague, he lived most of his life in Munich, Bavaria, which became in time the center of lithographic art. The story of the invention is one

---

* New York: Crown Publishers, Inc., 1970.

of a series of accidental discoveries growing out of Senefelder's ingenuity, industry, and need to save money. He had started out to be an actor, then a playwright, and it was to save the expense of having his plays printed that he taught himself printing and also etching on copper. Frequent errors in forming the reversed characters on the plate led him to devise a solution for use in rectifying the mistakes. He took the materials closest at hand—the wax with which he coated the plates previous to the etching, the soap with which he washed the ink from the plates, and the lampblack he used in preparing the printing ink. Thus, accidentally, he discovered the formula that forms the basis of all crayons and lithographic drawing ink.

To save the work of grinding and repolishing his copper plates, Senefelder experimented with a piece of stone, which led to another important element in lithography—a porous printing surface. One day while he was preparing to practice reverse writing, he responded to a household request for a laundry list by writing it down directly on the stone he had ready for etching. He used the composition that he had made for correction, and made another important discovery—it was not necessary to bring out the characters in relief with acid, as he had been doing. Simply writing on the stone with his special preparation brought the same results.

There were other experiments and other disappointments until he was established in 1798 as a lithographic printer in Munich. The principles he discovered and applied are basic still to the versatile process of lithography.

WOOD ENGRAVINGS

Wood engraving, which is often called the white-line method of engraving, has had as romantic a past as have aquatints and lithographs. It, too, was discovered in Europe and brought to this country through the devotion of one man, Alexander Anderson (1775–1870), who is credited not only with introducing the process in the early nineteenth century but with making ten thousand wood engravings of his own and teaching the method to others.

Many of Anderson's wood engravings are preserved in the New York Library's print collection. They show the wide range of purposes for which the process was used—from billheads to scholarly illustrations in many types of magazines.

Thomas Bewick, apprenticed to a jeweler in early eighteenth-century England, began making wood engravings by cutting his design on the end grain of a wood block, instead of on the plank side, as woodcuts had been made for centuries. Here, too, all the material except the design was cut away and ink applied to the relief surface of the design. This meant that the form was delineated by white lines where there was no ink, instead of black, and thus the name: white-

VIEW OF THE HUDSON FROM THE VICINITY OF WEST-POINT.

293. Romantic view of the Hudson from the vicinity of present-day West Point, a favorite locality with many artists. Littell, the creator of this scene, depicts one of the Hudson River steamers making its way among the shoals of small sailboats. *America Illustrated*

line engraving. This feature makes a wood engraving easily distinguishable by the collector.

Abel Brown was a contemporary wood engraver with Anderson. He has come to fame because of his historical *woodcut* (not a wood engraving) known as *View of Colonel Johnson's Engagement near the Moravian Town*. This does not really belong in the field of nautical antiques, but is worth mentioning to illustrate how the processes of the seventeenth and eighteenth centuries in the United States continued in use into the nineteenth, though much smaller numbers of prints were produced.

In the first half of the nineteenth century, wood engravings were used for all types of illustrations, and by mid-century they were making history in all the weeklies: *Harper's Weekly, Frank Leslie's Illustrated Newspaper, Appleton's Journal, Ballou's Pictorial Drawing-Room Companion,* and *Pearson's Magazine.*

Formerly these illustrations were thought of as reproductions. However, being a direct impression from the artist's engraving, they pass the test for an original print. Time has taken its toll. They are becoming scarce on the market, not because they were so in the beginning, but because of the natural tendency of pieces of paper to vanish from those spots where they must surely be! Have

294. Wood Engraving. A wood engraving is easily recognized because it is a relief process, and the ink is applied to the surface. This makes for white lines wherever the wood has been carved out. Look carefully at this wood engraving of *Sunset on Lake Michigan* (by Linton) and note the white lines running through the print. *Gleason's Pictorial Drawing-Room Companion, 1850*

295. Look out for the mackerel! What Maine fisherman didn't feel like shouting that warning when a newfangled steamship came by? This sketch by Joseph Becker made *Harper's Weekly* in 1851 and a collector's wall a hundred and some years later.

296. Portraits of ships appear in prints as well as in paintings. The stylized approach is apparent in this print from *Harper's Weekly*.

297. This wood engraving is a good example of the storytelling appeal a print can have. *Making Up Rafts on the Susquehanna River* depicts a way of life about which we have all too little information. Note the Erie Railroad train in the background. *America Illustrated*

MAKING UP RAFTS ON THE SUSQUEHANNA RIVER. A SCENE ON THE LINE OF THE ERIE RAILROAD

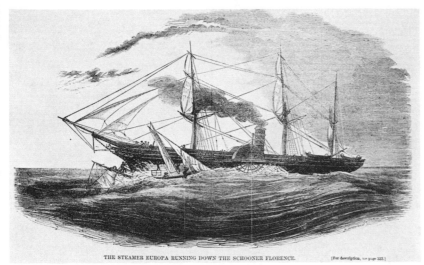

THE STEAMER EUROPA RUNNING DOWN THE SCHOONER FLORENCE. [For description, see page 255.]

298. Disaster prints have always had an appeal. Like this old wood-engraving of *The Steamer "Europa" Running Down the Schooner "Florence,"* they are dramatic, full of action, historical. *Gleason's Pictorial Drawing-Room Companion, 1850*

299. When the Civil War came, the steamers were converted into blockade runners, even warships. The prints that represent them are a collecting delight. *Gleason's Pictorial Drawing-Room Companion, 1850*

VIEW OF THE NAVY YARD, MEMPHIS, TENNESSEE, FROM THE ARKANSAS SHORE. [For description,

300. The Civil War is the only war of our history fully covered in engravings of all kinds. This print depicts the defeat of the *Alabama* by the *Kearsarge*. Isobel MacAnlay, Nova Scotia

THE UNITED STATES FLEET OFF FORT PICKENS, FLORIDA.—(See Page 246.)

301. Wood engravings in which every vessel is named, as they were in this one, have great interest for the collector of historic prints. Oftentimes they are the only record we have. Pictured here, from *Harper's Weekly,* is *The United States Fleet Off Fort Pickens, Florida.*

302. The steamship here leads a fleet of sailing ships with mortars off to war. No one dreamed that in the years ahead the steamship would lead—with no sailing ships to follow. This print, *Commander Porter's Mortar Flotilla,* also followed the practice of naming each vessel. *Harper's Weekly, 1861*

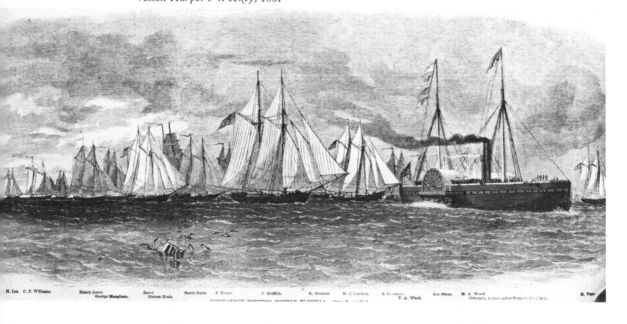

you ever tried to locate a week-old newspaper? Even one that you have put carefully aside? No wonder that the illustrated weeklies are difficult to find, and choice to possess, after a hundred years or more.

For many years Winslow Homer was an illustrator for *Harper's Weekly*. Unappreciated at the time as mere copies of his drawings, the pictures are now valuable as original prints. A Homer wood engraving of the *Alabama*, the ship that brought terror to Northern captains in the Civil War, was published in *Harper's Weekly* in 1863. A few years ago it could be purchased for twenty-five dollars. Today it is selling for one thousand dollars.

In various 1851 issues of *Gleason's Pictorial Drawing-Room Companion* are picturesque representations of the clippers *John Wade, Witch of the Waves,* and *Challenge.* They are accompanied by news items of interest to nautical enthusiasts, telling who built the ships, when, where; the dimensions of a vessel, its achievements, and especially its *speed*.

Whaling prints, considered difficult to find, may be in the weeklies. For example, you will find *A Whaling Station on the California Coast*, by Frenzeny, in an 1877 *Harper's Weekly*, and *The Perils of Whaling in the South Pacific* in an 1859 *Ballou's Pictorial Drawing-Room Companion*.

303. Lifesaving stations along the coast did much to cut the casualty list among seamen; swimmers along the beach were safeguarded by lifesaving precautions like these at Rockaway Beach. *Gleason's Pictorial Drawing-Room Companion, 1850*

LIFE-SAVING PRECAUTIONS AT ROCKAWAY BEACH.—[FROM A SKETCH BY C. A. KEETELS.]

305. *Boat Race on the Harlem River*, drawn by J. Davidson. This print gives something of the feeling of excitement that surrounded a boat race in the nineteenth century. Races were held almost every weekend from the time the ice broke until it formed again. (Oars and canopies may yet be found from this glamorized time.) Foreigners often marveled at the racing instinct of Americans. Even fishing boats returning from the Grand Banks raced for home, not just because the first one back would get the best price for his fish, but for the thrill of the race. Let two schooners come close in the open sea and what did they do? Race. No prize but pride in their vessels. *Harper's Weekly, 1875* ➤

GLEASON'S PICTORIAL DRAWING ROOM COMPANION.

LIGHT BOAT AT MINOT'S LEDGE.

304. The lightboat at Minot's Ledge is typical of many beacons that protected vessels in storm and wind on a treacherous coast. *Gleason's Pictorial Drawing-Room Companion, 1850*

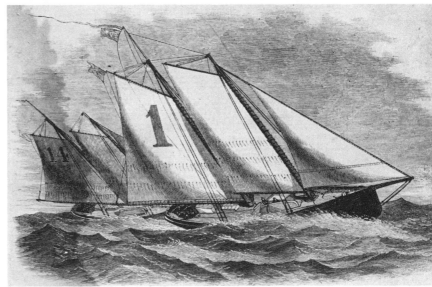

306. Sports enthusiasts
   and owners of small
   boats will find many
   delightful prints of
   races and activities
   of men in the 1850s.
   *Frank Leslie's Il-
   lustrated Newspaper,
   1866*

These magazine prints vary in size from a 6-by-9-inch impression to a full-page spread. They vary in quality, some hurried, some less skillful than others, but all of them breathe of bygone times, a quality dear to the hearts of collectors.

In the twenty-first century, some collector back from a moon trip may look at his two-hundred-year-old print of a steamship that half sailed, half steamed across the Atlantic, and smile over the words of Dr. Larchner, an En-

307. Etching, a means of getting beautiful renderings of a painting or scene, can be recognized by the deep contrasts of velvety black and other different tones. Shown here is an early Gordon Grant. Though born in 1875, Grant seems almost a contemporary. He reached back into the past with his art so that his etchings have an important place in many a nautical collection. His etching of the *Constitution* greatly aided Oliver Wendell Holmes in his battle to save that noble vessel. He made little dories and great ships live, so timelessly did he respond to the call of the sea. Most of Grant's works date from the 1930s, when he reached his height of popularity.

glish oceanographer, when the *Savannah* steamed into Liverpool Harbor in 1819: "Steam on the North Atlantic is merely a dream, and as to any idiotic project of making a voyage direct from Liverpool to New York under steam, I have no hesitation in saying one might as well talk of making such a voyage from here to the moon."

PHOTOGRAPHIC PRINTS

In these days of the instant image—the photograph in the living room at the moment it is being taken thousands of miles away—it is hard to realize how miraculous the photograph seemed to people living not much more than a century ago.

Museum directors are keenly aware of the value of photographs in preserving the past. Better than paintings, better than engravings, they show things just as they were. Directors I have interviewed invariably speak with pride and pleasure of their photographic collections. To historians doing research, and to plain lovers and collectors of nautical information and relics of our seafaring past, they are a never-ending source of delight.

The high price brought by ghoulish photographic records of the hanging of the Lincoln conspirators is one example of the interest in the field. Another example involves six old daguerreotypes recently found by a collector at a flea market. He thought the photographs were scenes of Washington, D.C., in the mid-nineteenth century, and sent them to the Smithsonian Institution for identification. The Smithsonian snapped them up at $2,000 apiece, a record price for daguerreotypes.

If you decide to scout around for old ship pictures and other nautical subjects, the period to watch for is roughly 1870 to 1910. The time to begin is *now*. Too many valuable photographs are lost through carelessness, thoughtless housecleaning, or ignorance of their potential value. Most families do not think of the pictures in the brass-clasped red-bound family album as historical documents with monetary and cultural values.

With the coming of the camera, sailors took pictures of the ships in which they sailed, just as in earlier days they sketched and whittled models of them. These photographs, when found, should be correlated with all the information you have: the name of the ship, its master, its owner, where it was launched, and its destination. Each bit of information adds to the importance of the picture. This holds true, too, in the case of the much-sought-after photographs of captains with the ships they sailed.

Artists drew, and newspapers reproduced, pictures of calamities, and amateur photographers were not far behind with their cameras. Such pictures as these may also be found in family albums. Riverboats, canalboats, and ferries, however, were so much a part of ordinary daily life that few bothered to photograph them. Often good pictures are found where the object was to photograph not the vessel but someone leaving on a trip.

A friend of mine who is an ardent photographer has a collection of photographs of old automobiles and locomotives. She has been so successful in running these down that I have urged her to start a collection of ship photographs.

With a little more foresight, we could have added some personal touches to the early twentieth-century nautical records of Buffalo and Lake Erie. Years ago we had an intelligent and photogenic cat named Collar. Because she was both curious and amiable, we would photograph her with the children in activities on excursions—boarding a trolley car, climbing on the wing of an airplane,

308. Icebound. Dramatic photographs like this one are always a prize. *Photograph courtesy of The Mariners Museum, Newport News, Virginia*

jumping into a canoe on the park lake. Our interest was in cat and children. Today it is the backgrounds that please and excite us. Why, I wonder, did we not take her to the Buffalo harbor where the D&C boats took off for Cleveland and Detroit, where ferries carried crowds to Fort Erie and Crystal Beach? Collar would have been most accommodating, but we never dreamed that in a short time, as history goes, the pleasure boats and excursions would no longer be commonplace, and the lake would be in need of rehabilitation from pollution.

The Bath Marine Museum has a collection of early photographic plates, gifts of the many shipyards in the vicinity. Over the years there have been two hundred such firms on the Kennebec River alone. The plates from which prints were made, prints of the vessels of Percy and Small, the great Seward shipbuilding company, and a score of others, furnish a standard of excellence for a collector's acquisition. Even though some of the plates may be chipped along the edges, the grandeur of the subjects cannot be dimmed.

Printmakers refer to both lithographic and photographic prints as surface prints, or technically as planographic prints. In the world of art, the value of a photographic print lies in its expression of an idea; in the world of the nautical collector, the value is in the presentation of a new version of a historic fact.

Photography can skillfully copy other forms of print, and you must be on your guard not to be deceived. The basis of a print is painting or drawing; of an old photographic print, it is the glass negative. Glass was used during the period in which you are seeking photographic prints. Film is the more recent development. Handle carefully the glass plates you find. You may be holding a small fortune.

If you are an amateur photographer, you might update history by making your own collection of pictures of historic vessels. Visit the maritime museums and seek out your models. Most of them have an old ship in snug harbor as part of their exhibits. You can bring to bear your own feeling for the subject in the particular artistic shot that you achieve. Gather and correlate the facts about the ships, and you grow in knowledge of the country's seagoing past as you build your own unusual collection.

309. The importance of a collection of maritime photographs is indicated in the pride all museums have in their photographic collections. A good photograph is almost as hard to obtain as a good print. *Photograph of Frederick P. Elkin by William T. Radcliffe, courtesy of The Mariners Museum, Newport News, Virginia*

310. The Horn's revenge. The mainmast was broken off at the deck, the yards tangled in rigging across the bulwarks, but the *Wavertree* brought its crew back to Port Stanley in the Falkland Islands, where this photograph was taken. Now it helps inspire the lovers of ships of yesteryear to help bring her and others back to life at South Street Seaport.

Two minor fields for collectors of nautical subjects are stereoscopic slides, which sometimes yield views of canalboats, side-wheelers, schooners, and the like, and postcards. Old postcards are more desirable, but I was much impressed with a collection made by a young friend. She had gathered attractive postcards in color from maritime museums. Classified by subject, they made an excellent, yet inexpensive, display. And quite unconsciously, she was training her eye to appreciate the best in ship models, figureheads, and old ships still afloat.

From the early 1600s to the nineteenth century, books too have illuminated the lore of the sea. They are now collectors' items of great value. Nor did this writing cease with our own century. Fascinating tales await those who turn to the historical aspect of our maritime heritage: books of great ships and great captains; of naval history in war and peace; of age of sail and of the great ocean liners. They serve as prods to further discovery, to make you look for graphic reminders of the past. They will also enlarge the borders of your mind and increase your knowledge of that heterogeneous land mass, the United States, which was founded by those who came by the sea—and is proudly lapped by its waves.

APPENDIX TO ACKNOWLEDGMENTS

MUSEUMS

Bath Marine Museum
    Bath, Maine

The Canal Museum
    Syracuse, New York

Columbia River Maritime Museum
    Astoria, Oregon

The Mariners Museum
    Newport News, Virginia

Mystic Seaport, Inc.
    Mystic, Connecticut

The New Brunswick Museum
        Saint John, New Brunswick
        Canada

Philadelphia Maritime Museum
        Philadelphia, Pennsylvania

San Francisco Maritime Museum
    San Francisco, California

South Street Seaport Museum
    New York, New York

United States Naval Academy
    Museum
    Annapolis, Maryland

DEALERS

Helene Barry Antiques
    Kew Gardens, New York
    Dealer: Mr. & Mrs. Barry Shatoff

John Bihler & Henry Coger Antiques
    Ashley Falls, Massachusetts

Cornelia Black
    Westchester Commission Mart
    Peekskill, New York

Ronald Bourgeault Antiques
    Salem, Massachusetts

Brainstorm Farm Antiques
    Randolph, Vermont

Lake View Galleries
    Lake View, New York

Rita Merdinger
    Ridgewood, New York

Fenton D. Moore
    Buffalo, New York

Eleanor Mulligan
    Harrington Park, New Jersey

Old Toll House Antiques
    Westbury, New York
    Dealer: Thomas Cafaro

Gary C. Cole
New York, New York

The Herald Corbins
Three Ravens
Falls Village, Connecticut

Allan L. Daniel
New York, New York

Harris Diamant
Eris Antiques, Inc.
New York, New York

Gibson's Antiques
Lakeview, New York

Good, Hutchinson & Ass.
Tolland, Massachusetts

Nina Hellman Antiques
Bedford, New York

A.S. Hewitt—The Plaza
Locust Valley, New York
Dealer: Ellen Fales Lomasnay

Hilbert Brothers
New Canaan, Connecticut

Hirschl & Adler Galleries
New York, New York

Valdemar Jacobson
Cold Springs, New York

John B. Kiener III
Lancaster, New York

Karl and Gladys Kranz
Hamburg, New York

Arlene and Richard Orcutt
Stamford, Connecticut

John A. Reardon
Andover, Massachusetts

Bern C. Ritchie & Co.
Winnetka (Hubbard Woods),
Illinois

Charles B. Smith Antiques
Philadelphia, Pennsylvania

Patricia and Sanford Smith Galleries
New York, New York

Kenneth E. Snow Antiques
Newburyport, Massachusetts

The Stradlings
New York, New York

Frank F. Sylvia Antiques
Nantucket, Massachusetts

Turner & Loughlin
Wilton, Connecticut

Village Green Antiques
Richland, Michigan

Barbara Vollmeck
The Ante Shop
Pacific, Missouri

Roger G. Williams
Old Curiosity Shop
Newbury, Massachusetts

LIGHT ON YOUR COLLECTION
A Bibliography

IN NO OTHER FIELD OF collecting does research release so golden a light as in that of nautical antiques. The patina of your treasures will take on an added glow from your own expanding knowledge of their history. Worm-eaten pieces of wood turn pure gold in fancy as their stories become known through reading and study.

Turn first to the libraries with their well-indexed bibliographies listing books upon books about ships and the ways of seafaring men. Here identification becomes a fascinating trail—and also a long and time-consuming one.

If one is in a hurry to get the feel of a subject, a quick and productive route is through several excellent periodicals devoted to the subject of antiques in general. *The Magazine Antiques* has, through the years, been the repository of many articles about nautical antiques. Well-illustrated, scholarly, and readable, they cover such diverse specialties as scrimshaw, ship models, paintings and prints, the China trade, lamps and lanterns, maps, receipts. A great many libraries, even in small cities, have bound volumes of the magazine. Subjects are well indexed. You will have no difficuly in running down your leads.

Other magazines of interest to the nautical collector are *Yankee Magazine* and *Down East.* The former has the wider base of New England; the latter is centered on matters of particular interest to Maine and its admirers. Both turn the floodlight of the past on the events of a region and make history into fascinating new reading for devotees of ships, the sea, and land-based nautical operations. Of interest too are such magazines as *Hobbies, The Antique Trader, Spinning Wheel,* and the *Antiques Journal.*

Bulletins of museums, particularly of nautical, marine, or maritime museums, contain the latest information on the field in America. The *Nautical Museum Directory,* published by Quadrant Press, Inc., lists nautical museums and preserved vessels in the United States and Canada. Collectors should consider it a duty and a privilege to join and support as many as possible of these comparatively recent storehouses of marine artifacts and history.

Designed to make a significant contribution to American history is the recent project of the Mystic Seaport and Wesleyan University Press. Titled *The American Maritime Library,* the collected works include to date the following volumes:

Albion, Robert G.; Baker, William A.; and Labaree, Benjamin W. *New England and the Sea*

Baughman, James P. *Maritime Enterprise*

Beck, Horace. *Folklore and the Seas*

Ely, Ben-Ezra Stiles. *There She Blows.* A narrative of a whaling voyage in the Indian and South Atlantic oceans

Leavitt, John F. *Wake of the Coasters*

Mjelde, Michael J. *Glory of the Seas*

The Peabody Museum has sponsored a long list of books, some in conjunction with Harvard University, others with the Boston Public Library. Among them the nautical collector is sure to find his own particular specialty. Information on the publications may be obtained from The Peabody Museum, Salem, Massachusetts, 01970.

Choosing general books is somewhat more difficult. Many abound in the history of antiques, but only incidentally in the collecting of marine artifacts. The late Helen Comstock did great service to all lovers of things in editing *The Concise Encyclopedia of American Antiques.* In it, practically all the important aspects of American nautical antiques are covered by well-known authorities. Accompanying bibliographies furnish leads for exploration in each field.

There is an underlying unity in the art of the sea. Though symbols may differ among nations, the seaman's concepts are universal. By understanding the mariner's background the world over, we can better understand our own. Two books along these lines are well worth reading:

Hasen, Hans Jergen. *Arts and the Seafarer.* Translated by James and Inge Moore. New York: The Viking Press, 1968.

Frere-Cook, Gervis, ed. *The Decorative Arts of the Mariner.* Boston and Toronto: Little Brown and Company, 1966.

In Neale Haley's *The Schooner Era, A Lost Epic in History* (A. S. Barnes & Company, Inc., 1972), there is an enlightening chapter on nautical antiques. The book also contains hitherto little known information about the schooners that sailed along the eastern and western coasts, with well-written stories that make it excellent reading.

INDEX